DOWN THE SLIPPERY SLOPE:
ARGUING IN APPLIED ETHICS

Down the Slippery Slope

ARGUING IN APPLIED ETHICS

David Lamb

CROOM HELM
London • New York • Sydney

© 1988 David Lamb
Croom Helm Ltd, Provident House,
Burrell Row, Beckenham, Kent, BR3 1AT

Croom Helm Australia, 44 – 50 Waterloo Road,
North Ryde, 2113, New South Wales

Published in the USA by
Croom Helm
in association with Methuen, Inc.
29 West 35th Street,
New York, NY 10001

British Library Cataloguing in Publication Data

Lamb, David, *1942 –*
    Down the slippery slope: Arguing in Applied Ethics
    1. Euthanasia—Moral and ethical aspects
    2. Abortion—Moral and ethical aspects
    I. Title
    174'.24   R726
    ISBN 0-7099-4166-8

Library of Congress Cataloguing in Publication Data
ISBN 0-7099-4166-8

Printed and bound in Great Britain by Mackays of Chatham Ltd, Kent

Contents

Acknowledgements

This book has developed out of a series of lectures and papers given to philosophy meetings at the universities of Manchester, Sussex, Southampton, Sheffield, Kent, and Cardiff, and I am grateful to the organisers of these meetings for the opportunity to air the views expressed here in public. I would like to include a special note of thanks to Harry Lesser and Gavin Fairbourne who invited me to address meetings of the Northern Universities Association for Philosophy, and to Don Evans, Director of the MA course in Medical Ethics at the University of Cardiff, who invited me to defend my interpretation of the slippery slope argument at seminars held at Gregynog Hall, Powys, Wales, which is one of the most enjoyable locations in the Principality for philosophical discussion. Thanks also to the organisers of the philosophy programme at the Brewery Arts Centre in Kendal, who kindly invited me to address their members on topics relevant to this book, and to Sadie Plant who invited me to participate in her philosophy teaching programme in the Manchester area. For research assistance on this project and many others I would like to thank Heather Draper. For valuable help in the preparation of the manuscript I would like to thank Rosemary Sheldon for critical and helpful comments on early drafts, and Deborah Carlisle for her secretarial assistance throughout the project. Finally, I would like to thank Bill Ireson for all of his assistance in the final stages of preparation.

Introduction

The 'slippery slope' argument can be found in all areas of policy-making. It has numerous descriptions and appears in many guises. Sometimes it is called the 'thin end of the wedge argument' or 'the primrose path argument', 'the domino theory', 'the floodgates', 'the tip of the iceberg', 'the camel's nose in the tent argument', 'the bald man argument', or the '*sorites* or heap argument'. These metaphors are suggestive of a series of gradual steps from an acceptable to an unacceptable position, where it is difficult to determine the exact point at which the crucial transition is made. The most common employment of the slippery slope argument is in the form of a rejection of a newly proposed moral or legal boundary where the objection is not merely directed at the proposal *per se* but to the undesirable consequences which may arise out of it. Opponents of the slope argument frequently dismiss this version as an indirect argument which illicitly confuses the possible with the actual. Nevertheless, policy-makers use versions of the slippery slope argument frequently and it is one of the central arguments in the ethics of medical care. In the context of the rapid changes in medical technology during the past two decades, where traditional value-systems have been confronted with new dilemmas and options hitherto considered inconceivable, an examination of the slope argument must be at the forefront of ethical concern.

Opponents of voluntary termination of pregnancy and euthanasia frequently employ versions of the slope argument in an appeal to what are seen as the predictable long-range consequences of the legalisation of these practices. It has been argued that the legalisation of voluntarily terminated pregnancy or euthanasia for humane reasons would open the door to a more callous disregard for human life. Opponents of legalised abortions and euthanasia have predicted that further inevitable steps would include the killing of mentally-retarded children, those whose maintenance is costly, the aged, senile, and those who are socially undesirable. What might initially appear as innocent and humane steps, it is argued, might even lead to the killing of those who are sometimes regarded as politically and racially undesirable. It is in this way that the parade of Nazi atrocities is frequently brought out to block off any attempt to introduce the legalisation of accelerated death.

It is quite obvious that the slope argument can be abused. Taken out of context it can be shown as a ridiculous argument which could be employed against any proposed improvement to human welfare. For this reason any serious appraisal of the slope argument must distinguish between its valid and invalid applications. It is clear that legislators and physicians and others concerned with human welfare are guided in their actions by a resistance to proposals which can be interpreted as steps down a slippery slope. Yet many philosophers have dismissed the slope argument as a method of fallacious reasoning. Notwithstanding some obvious objections to the slope argument it will be argued, throughout the following chapters, that its opponents have not provided a proper refutation and, when properly understood, there is an important place for an appeal to slippery slopes in ethical decision-making.

One of the reasons why the slope argument has been so frequently misunderstood is that because much of what passes for philosophical argument and refutation is conducted in an abstract setting, where an appeal to certain aspects of an argument's formal properties may be all that is required for a philosopher to consider it to have been adequately refuted. But the problem is that the slope argument appears in many forms and its validity may depend upon the context in which it is employed. It follows that an adequate assessment of the slope argument demands an inquiry into the contexts in which it occurs together with an appraisal of the potential effects of the proposal on some of our more fundamental moral beliefs. As Kamisar (1958, p. 1031) observes: 'Whether the first step is precarious, is perilous, is worth taking, rests in part on what the second step is likely to be.'

In Chapter 1 a general examination of the slippery slope argument will be conducted, and in the following chapters various uses of the slope argument will be assessed in the contexts in which they appear. Chapter 2 examines the function of the parade of Nazi horrors in the slope argument and assesses the relevance of the Nazi analogy for contemporary ethical decision-making. In Chapter 3 the slippery slope objections to proposals which entail a departure from the sanctity of life principle are examined. Chapter 4 examines the prediction that any further extensions to legally permissible forms of killing may contribute to a situation where killing is contagious, and the issue of voluntary euthanasia — frequently considered to be immune from slippery slope objections

— will be examined in Chapter 5. In Chapter 6 a crucial distinction is outlined between voluntary euthanasia and the right to remove oneself from certain kinds of life-sustaining therapy. Other arguments in favour of accelerated death will be assessed in Chapters 7 and 8 where arguments in favour of beneficient euthanasia and euthanasia based on cost-benefit considerations will be assessed. Chapters 9 and 10 assess the relevance of the slope argument in the context of recent proposals regarding *in vitro* fertilisation techniques and research on embryos and proposals to extend criteria for the voluntary termination of pregnancy. The Conclusion expresses the author's view that, properly understood, the slope argument is essential to the ethics of medical care in an era of rapid technological intervention.

1

The Slippery Slope Argument

A degree of intuitive plausibility in the slope or wedge argument can be seen in the following example. In 1967, a black murderer, Aaron Mitchell, was denied an appeal for clemency by Ronald Reagan, who was at that time the Governor of California. Following Mitchell's execution there was a moratorium on state executions until 1977, when the convicted murderer, Gary Gilmore, won the right to be executed by a firing squad in the State of Utah. Since Gilmore's death there have been scores of other executions and, given the public appetite for capital punishment (72 per cent in the USA in favour according to a recent opinion poll), it is plausible to predict that, all things being equal, the number of state executions will continue to increase.

Now the fact that Gilmore's execution was made possible because he had voluntarily demanded execution and went to great lengths to achieve it (including a suicide attempt) is largely ignored or considered irrelevant by those who saw it as a means of reintroducing the programme of state executions. What might have appeared to some as an exceptional case, involving a newly proposed moral boundary wherein it is permissible to execute convicted murderers who have clearly demonstrated a rational desire to die, has since been passed over as a step towards full restoration of the death penalty. If capital punishment is fully restored in the USA and radically extended it will not be necessary to show that Gilmore's death was causally responsible, but it is nevertheless plausible to suggest that his execution is an example of a first step on a slippery slope.

As this example indicates, the first step on the slope need not determine further developments, but it can be said that it facilitates such developments when there is a social situation in which they are likely to achieve approval.

The Gilmore case draws attention to an important qualification to the slippery slope argument. It was not merely the fact that Gilmore fulfilled his desire for the death penalty which lead to the initial steps down the slope to a full restoration of capital punishment, for it required the additional social fact that such a process is likely to occur. For a slope argument to have any significance the situation must be such that people must have some reason to move down the slope from one step to another. Proposals to curtail current proposals by reference to future possible abuses have little force if they refer only to the merely possible. The situation must exhibit other features for the slope argument to have any relevance. In the Gilmore case there was a strong body of opinion in favour of a return to capital punishment, which only required a precedent. From the standpoint of the outright opponent of capital punishment, given a plausible expectation of further steps down the slope, there would be some justification in the attempt to forestall the first step.

In many discussions concerning proposals to legalise euthanasia the slope or wedge argument is invoked by those who fear serious abuse of the original proposal. An extreme form of the argument appears in the objections to the legalisation of voluntary euthanasia, expressed by Bishop Joseph V. Sullivan:

> If voluntary euthanasia were legalized, there is good reason to believe that at a later date another bill for compulsory euthanasia would be legalized. Once the respect for human life is so low that an innocent person may be killed directly even at his own request, compulsory euthanasia will necessarily be very near. This could lead easily to killing all incurable cancer patients, the aged who are a public care, wounded soldiers, all deformed children, the mentally afflicted, and so on. Before long the danger would be at the door of every citizen.
>
> Once a man is permitted on his own authority to kill an innocent person directly, there is no way of stopping the advancement of that wedge. There exists no longer any rational grounds for saying that the wedge can advance so far and no further. Once the exception has been made it is too late; hence the grave reason why no exception may be allowed. That is why euthanasia under any circumstances must be condemned. (Cited by Rachels, 1986, p. 171.)

James Rachels (1986) cites these objections to voluntary euthanasia as examples to illustrate what he sees as the fallacious reasoning behind the slope or wedge argument. Sullivan's objection to voluntary euthanasia, argues Rachels, runs together two distinct versions of the slope argument, the *logical* and the *psychological*, neither of which provide acceptable grounds for the prohibition of euthanasia.

The logical version

According to Rachels the logical version argues that once one form of euthanasia is accepted then one is logically committed to an approval of euthanasia in other cases. As Sullivan says 'there exists no longer any rational grounds for saying that the wedge can advance so far and no further'. But Rachels disagrees and points out 'there are rational grounds for distinguishing between the man in agony who wants to die and other cases, such as that of an old infirm person who does not want to die'. (1986, p. 173.) For example, the former wants death, the latter does not; one is suffering terribly, the other is not. That such rational distinctions can be made, argues Rachels, reveals the inadequacy of the logical version of the slope argument. 'It does not', he says, 'provide good grounds for thinking that euthanasia ought to be legally prohibited'. (1986, p. 173.)

But has Rachels really overcome the slope objection to voluntary euthanasia? It may be that Sullivan has overstated the prediction of horrible results, especially with his references to the compulsory killing of wounded soldiers, children and charity patients. But what lies behind Sullivan's rhetoric is a warning about reasoning with loose concepts, against moving from a moral absolute with determinate boundaries to a new rule which rests upon indeterminate concepts such as 'voluntary', 'wants' and 'requests', and non-quantifiable states such as 'agony' and 'suffering', all of which can be stretched, loosely interpreted or misunderstood, such that they might even admit of some of the horrible results predicted by Sullivan. To take one example: the concept of 'voluntary' might be stretched to apply to the killing of a wounded soldier who does not want to die but has nevertheless freely volunteered for a mission the success of which depends on not leaving any wounded behind for the enemy to interrogate. It could be argued that in one sense his death was voluntary. At least such a position is open to argument. And that is the point behind the logical version of the slope argument: once clear cut absolutes are replaced by indeterminate concepts moral boundaries can become a playgound for sophistry.

The psychological version

According to this version, argues Rachels, 'once certain practices are accepted, *people shall in fact* go on to accept other, more questionable practices'. (1986, p. 173.) This version involves an empirical prediction about what people shall do, and is therefore not about what they would be logically committed to believing. (Frequently this version takes the form of a prediction about the alleged contagiousness of killing, which will be examined in Chapter 4.)

Once defined as an empirical prediction, Rachels maintains that the slope argument can be refuted with evidence to the contrary. Historical and anthropological evidence is therefore cited in order to show that killing in one context does not lead to killing in another. Infanticide amongst the ancient Greeks and parenticide amongst certain eskimo communities, so it is argued, did not lead to more widespread forms of killing.

Yet this evidence does not satisfactorily displace the slippery slope objections to voluntary euthanasia, for it can always be asserted that any newly proposed moral boundary can be open to empirical confusion, misunderstanding, and abuse. Rachels is, however, aware of the possible abuses of legalised euthanasia and concedes that once legalised there could be no guarantee against abuse. But he supports the proposal maintaining that 'the crucial issue is whether the evil of the abuses would be so great as to outweigh the benefit of the practice'. (1986, p. 175.) For Rachels the evils of abuse in the present legislation outweigh the evils of potential abuse if euthanasia were legalised. It would seem that the success or failure of the slope argument turns on the respective predictions of greater or lesser abuse. Accordingly, in some cases the slope objection would be correct and in other cases it would be incorrect; the status of the argument would be contingent.

We shall have more to say in Chapter 5 about the employment of a consequentialist balance sheet with regard to the legalisation of voluntary euthanasia, but it must be stressed that any argument which draws attention to possible abuses deserves a prominent place amongst the priorities of those who propose new moral and legal boundaries. Accordingly, the slippery slope objection to euthanasia is not refuted with reference to an excess of abuses in present practices: if it forces the proposer of a new moral boundary to consider potential abuse it must serve as an important check against ill-thought out proposals. Thus in any debate on euthanasia the prediction of abuse calls for more consideration about the *kind* of abuse that might occur. This would include predictions about the risk of killing those who do not want to die. The present system which prohibits euthanasia may be open to the kind of abuse where life is prolonged without good reason. But the abuse obviously ends when death naturally occurs. There is a natural limit to this kind of abuse. But there is no possible procedure for dealing with an abuse which involves an unwanted death. That kind of abuse is irreversible. In such cases the slope argument is a constant reminder that the finality of death demands the kind of discussion that can be formulated only in clear, definable and unambiguous terms.

The foregoing discussion has indicated that the slippery slope argument depends upon a combination of two factors. The first is that there is an agreement over the alleged prediction of abuses and a consensus that these end results would be undesirable. Second, the slope argument functions as a warning against reasoning to newly proposed moral boundaries with loose concepts. The first factor is bound up with *predictable* consequences whereas the latter is bound up with *unpredictable* consequences.

Bernard Williams (1985) has captured these features in his distinction between *the horrible results argument* and the *arbitrary results argument*.

The horrible results argument

The status of this argument depends primarily on agreement regarding the horrible nature of the end result. For example, an objection to the proposals for experiments on embryos might proceed as follows: at present there is a limit on the period of time allowed for experiments on embryos, but eventually it might be extended to cover experiments on developed embryos. For the slope argument to get off the ground in this case it would have to depend upon prior agreement regarding the unacceptability of experiments on more developed embryos. In some versions of the argument the horrible results may be extended to the point where they will include reference to horrible actions which would be condemned by any rational member of a moral community. It is in this context that the parade of Nazi atrocities may be introduced as a possible horrible result.

The arbitrary results argument

The second form of argument does not depend upon prior agreement regarding the horrible nature of the results, but rather on the prediction that once having stepped on the slope the stopping point will be arbitrary. To illustrate this point Williams offers the following example:

> Suppose that some tax relief or similar benefit be extended to couples who are not married. Someone might not object to the very idea of the relief going to unmarried couples, but nevertheless argue that the only non-arbitrary line that could be drawn was between the married couples and the unmarried, and that as soon as any unmarried couple was allowed the benefit, there would be too many arbitrary discriminations to be made. (Williams, 1985, p. 127.)

As the above remarks indicate, this version of the slope argument serves as a warning against reasoning with loose concepts.

Reasoning with loose concepts

Although it is important to retain Williams's distinction between the two forms of the slope argument, in practice they are frequently run together. This is acceptable so long as the argument refers to a situation where there is both agreement over the horrible results and a prediction of an arbitrary boundary between the acceptable and the unacceptable. Confusion occurs when an attempt to rebut the arbitrary results version is made with arguments designed exclusively for a rebuttal of the horrible results version. For example, a slippery slope prediction of arbitrary results would not be invalidated by a reassurance that the consequences need not be disastrous. An objection to the termination of certain expensive forms of therapy would not be invalidated

6

by means of an assurance that such a course would not necessarily lead to a widespread programme of involuntary euthanasia. For in this case the slippery slope objection might have been simply aimed at the arbitrary nature of any proposal which depends on an inherently loose concept such as 'expensive therapy'.

The slippery slope warning about reasoning with loose concepts deserves further elaboration. It draws attention to a feature of argument which is often overlooked by those who may not have given serious attention to the kinds of arguments involved in proposals to create new moral boundaries. Logical analysis is clearly relevant to the formulation of moral arguments, but it can only deal with determinate concepts. The slope argument is a reminder of the risk of such a slide into indeterminacy. Max Black has drawn attention to the problem of reasoning with loose concepts:

> In learning how to use logical principles in connection with ordinary concepts, I suggest, we have to understand the general agreement that only *determinate* statements shall be held subject to the rules. (Similarly, the principles of geometry are intended to apply only to *rigid* bodies; precise concepts are to logic, one might say, as rigid bodies to geometry.) It follows that whenever we use logical principles in reasoning with loose concepts we must be on the alert for gradual slides into indeterminacy. (Black, 1970, p. 11.)

When reasoning with loose concepts it has to be recognised that definitions and descriptions are inherently arbitrary. Thus, in the case of the *sorites* (or heap or bald man) form of the slippery slope argument, it is self-evident that there is no precise moment when the last additional grain of sand satisfies rigid criteria for the definition of a 'heap'. We simply judge when we have an idea that certain words, like 'heap' or 'baldness' can be used. Likewise, although the concept of death can and ought to be precisely defined (Lamb, 1985), there is no such precision obtainable in concepts relating to the quality of life. This would be a matter of making decisions according to the contexts, where no absolute guidelines can be laid down. According to Black:

> Just as the sharpest knife eventually fails to cut, so even the best-defined empirical concept eventually fails to discriminate — and there is nothing surprising about that. I have to *decide* when to call a halt (influenced, of course, by the practical or

theoretical interests at stake) just because there are not and cannot be any rules for stopping. (Black, 1970, pp. 11 – 12.)

When a slippery slope has been properly identified there are no rules for drawing to a halt at any particular stage. This point can be illustrated by developing one of Black's examples concerning the prohibition of 'take backs' in the game of chess. (Black, 1970, pp. 12 – 130.) Thus, if I play chess with a child we may allow each other to 'take back' bad moves. But if we use this privilege too often the game would be impossible to play. That would be, from the standpoint of the game, an agreed 'horrible end result' of the slope. Now there may be very good reasons to allow several 'take backs'. They may be helpful for the purpose of instruction. The problem occurs when we try to introduce a rule which allows 'take backs' under 'appropriate circumstances', and expect that rule to be incorporated into the game. Should the rule specify the number of 'take backs' per game? Exactly what conditions should be included in the critera for permissible 'take backs'? For the game that was formerly played was one that *absolutely* forbad 'take backs', and recognised that wrongness of so doing. Moreover, players who allowed 'take backs' would acknowledge the wrongness and would have probably indicated that it was an exceptional case. For in actual practice loosely agreed expectations may be tailored to suit the situation. In fact it would be the looseness of the practice of allowing 'take backs' (whilst acknowledging their wrongness) which guarantees the sense of the game. Accordingly 'take backs' do not require definition, and criteria for allowing them need not be incorporated into the rules of the game.

Applying this kind of reasoning to slippery slope objections to euthanasia one might discover that certain ways of accelerating the dying process might be morally acceptable according to the situation, just as 'take backs' might be accepted in a chess game. But it is an entirely different matter when an attempt to incorporate euthanasia into medical practice is made. For here precise definitions and guidelines would have to be formulated. But as exponents of the slippery slope argument rightly point out this would do fundamental damage to the existing sense of therapy and care; these concepts would be hedged with qualifications and uncertainty. It may be that in practice some physicians have accelerated the dying process just as some chess players have broken the rule against 'take backs'. They might be rightly accused of subscribing to double standards in that they subscribe to certain principles but occasionally break them. But holding double standards where one of which is clearly formulated and essential to the activity in question is preferable to standards which are imprecise and subject to constant revision and misunderstanding.

The strengths of slippery slope objections are two-fold; given an appropriate social situation they force a discussion of potential abuse of certain newly proposed moral boundaries, and draw attention to the error of analysing indeterminate concepts with methods which are only appropriate for the analysis of determinate concepts. It is important to be precise about concepts we can be precise about and to be careful to recognise concepts we cannot be precise about.

2

It Started from Small Beginnings

The most extreme example of a slide into moral depravity is the Nazi euthanasia programme which originated in discussions on mercy killing in 1933. By 1936 it was so widely discussed that additional proposals for the physically and socially unfit were suggested only incidentally in an article published by an official German medical journal. The actual programme was launched with a particular case involving the father of a deformed infant who asked Hitler for permission to have the child killed on merciful grounds. Hitler replied that if an investigation verified the facts of the case as presented by the father he would personally instruct physicians to carry out the father's request. Furthermore, Hitler assured him that he would be exempt from any criminal responsibility. But, as the historian, Lucy Dawidowicz, points out, these merciful intentions were merely a ploy to implement a more extensive programme of killing:

> Hitler used this particular case to embark on the programme he had long had in mind and indeed which he had already sketched out in *Mein Kampf*, a programme of radical eugenics, which destroyed life that did not meet 'Aryan' racial standards. (Dawidowicz, 1976, p. 3.)

The plea on behalf of the deformed child gave Hitler an opportunity to insert the 'thin end of the wedge'. In *Mein Kampf* he had written that the Volkish state must use the most modern medical means to 'declare unfit for propagation all those who are in any way visibly sick, all who have inherited a disease and can therefore pass it on'. (Cited by Dawidowicz, 1976, p. 9.) According to

Telford Taylor, who was the chief counsel for the prosecution at the Nuremberg War Crimes trial, the insertion of the wedge actually took place on the first day of the Second World War, on 1 September 1939, when Hitler addressed Karl Brandt, who was the official head of the German medical profession, as follows:

> Reichsleiter Bouhler and Dr Brandt M.D. are charged with the responsibility of enlarging the authority of certain physicians to be designated by me in such a manner that persons who, according to human judgement, are incurably sick may, upon the most careful diagnosis of their medical condition, be accorded a mercy death. (Cited by Taylor, 1976, p. 9.)

In fact the order was issued in October and predated, but there is little doubt that this was the beginning of the Nazi euthanasia programme. Telford Taylor has pointed out that the euthanasia programme was more of an 'improvised affair' than many publications following Nuremberg indicate. (Taylor, 1976, p. 4.) This suggests that each step down the slope may not have been as carefully orchestrated as it has sometimes been maintained, but there is little doubt that the Nazis saw the initial steps as part of a wider programme.

The categories for extermination included the mentally-defective, psychotics (including schizophrenics), epileptics, those suffering from various infirmities of old age and organic neurological disorders such as infantile paralysis, Parkinsonism, multiple-sclerosis, and brain tumours. In the initial stages Jews were excluded from this privilege of 'merciful release'. Charities were utilised to give respectability to the programme: the 'Charitable Transport Company for the Sick' delivered patients to extermination centres, and institutions such as the 'Charitable Foundation for Institutional Care' collected the cost of exterminations from relatives.

Altogether 275,000 people were exterminated in this programme. Hitler called them 'useless eaters'. There was little evidence of resistance; although in a letter to the Court of Appeals in Frankfurt, December 1939, there was a demand for 'legislative regulations providing some orderly method that will ensure especially that the aged feeble-minded are not included in the programme'. (Alexander, 1949, p. 40.) These demands, however, can be seen as a particularly notorious way of legitimising the insertion of the wedge, since shifting the area of discussion to the limits of a programme can be a very effective means of establishing its plausibility; and in this case the scope for moral concern was confined to particular cases rather than the programme as a whole.

Leo Alexander, who investigated crimes committed by members of the German medical professsion, is a forceful exponent of the slope argument. His comments on the crimes committed by German physicians during the Third Reich do not merely refer to the 'horrible results' of the Nazi slope, but draw attention to the 'arbitrary results' entailed in the judgement that 'some lives are not worth living':

> Whatever proportions these crimes finally assumed, it became evident to all who investigated them that they had started from small beginnings. The beginnings at first were merely a subtle shift in emphasis in the basic attitude of the physicians. It started with the acceptance of an attitude, basic in the euthanasia movement, that there is such a thing as a life not worthy to be lived. This attitude in its early stages concerned itself merely with the severely and chronically sick. Gradually the sphere of those to be included in this category was enlarged to encompass the socially unproductive, the ideologically unwanted and finally all non-Germans. But it is important to realise that the infinitely small wedged-in lever from which this entire trend of mind received its impetus was the attitude towards the non-rehabitable sick. (Alexander, 1949, p. 44.)

It is significant that Alexander emphasises a shift in attitudes among physicians towards the non-rehabitable. In a detailed study of the Nazi euthanasia programme Frederic Wertham (1980) has drawn attention to support among psychiatrists. Far from being the result of a direct order from Hitler, says Wertham:

> The reality was very different. There was no law and no such order. The tragedy is that the psychiatrists did not have to have an order. They acted on their own. They were not carrying out a death sentence pronounced by somebody else. They were the legislators who laid down the rules for deciding who was to die; they were the administrators who worked out the procedures, provided the patients and the places, and decided the methods of killing; they pronounced a sentence of life or death in every individual case; they were the executioners

who carried the sentences out — without being coerced to do so — surrendered their patients to be killed in other institutions; they supervised and often watched their slow deaths. (Wertham, 1980, p. 614.)

Alexander offers several illustrations which indicate how the German people and their medical authorities travelled from euthanasia to the extermination camps. One example involved the introduction of ethical dilemmas with in-built presuppositions of social utility. Schoolchildren were set mathematical problems, such as, 'how many new housing units could be built and how many marriage allowance loans could be given to newly-wed couples for the amount of money it cost the state to care for the crippled, the criminal, and the insane?' (Alexander, 1949, p. 39.) Having established a degree of plausibility for extermination on cost-benefit terms the criteria for the assessment of lives that were not worth living was extended to include the non-rehabitable and those 'unfit for work'. The concept of 'non-rehabitable' is sufficiently undetermined for its scope to be extended almost indefinitely. It might include various comatose states, severe physical injuries or, from a racist perspective, non-Aryans. Fairly soon the euthanasia programme was to become the nucleus of plans to exterminate Jews and Poles, and to cut down the Russian population by 30 million.

Another route down the slope lay in the brutalisation of medical workers. Dr. Hallerworden, who received 500 brains from extermination centres, recalled that:

The worst thing about the business was that it produced a certain brutalization of nursing personnel. They got to simply picking out those whom they did not like, and the doctors had so many patients that they did not know them, and put their names on the list. (Alexander, 1949, p. 40.)

Brutalisation of this kind went hand-in-hand with a market concept of human life. A vivid example of this can be seen in the letters sent by the I. G. Farben chemical trust to the camp at Auschwitz.

In contemplation of your experiments with a new soporific drug, we would appreciate your producing for us a number of women . . . We received your answer but consider the price of 200 marks a woman excessive. We propose to pay not more than 170 marks a head. If agreeable, we will take possession of the women. We need approximately 150 . . . Received the order of 150 women. Despite their emaciated condition, they were found satisfactory. We shall keep you posted on developments concerning the experiment . . . The tests were made. All subjects died. We shall contact you shortly on the subject of a new load. (Cited by Glover, 1977, p. 58.)

Apart from biased presentations of ethical dilemmas and the brutalisation of medical personnel, the most significant factor in the Nazi-inspired slide into moral depravity was the attempt to restrict the concept of medical care to rehabilitation. It was to the credit of Dutch physicians in occupied Holland that they recognised and resisted this step. When they attempted to draw Dutch physicians into the orbit of German medical practice, the Nazis did not ask them to kill their patients. Their request was couched in more acceptable terms. Superficially, the following statement from the Reich Commissioner for the Netherlands is harmless:

It is the duty of the doctor, through advice and effort, conscientiously and to his best ability, to assist as helper the person entrusted to his care in the maintenance, improvement and re-establishment of his vitality, physical efficiency and health. The accomplishment of this duty is a public task. (Cited by Alexander, 1949, p. 45.)

The apparent innocence of this statement obscured the fact that it called for the concentration of efforts on rehabilitation of the sick for useful labour and the abolition of medical confidentiality. This step was resisted despite the arrest of 100 Dutch physicians who were sent to concentration camps. Not a single euthanasia or non-therapeutic sterilisation was recommended or participated in by Dutch physicians. Alexander attributes this to a refusal to step on to the slope. 'It is the first innocent step away from principle', he says, 'that frequently decides a career of crime. Coercion begins in microscopic proportions.' (Alexander, 1949, p. 40.) These remarks serve as a warning of very grave dangers which follow the acceptance of the belief that only those with an optimistic prognosis should receive the best treatment. For Alexander, the path down the slope is one of logical necessity:

From the attitude of easing patients with chronic diseases away from the doors of the best type of treatment facilities available to the actual despatching of such patients to the killing centres is a long but nevertheless logical step. (Ibid., p. 45.)

There are few philosophers today who accept Alexander's employment of the slope argument, and there is considerable scepticism with regard to the value of drawing parallels between contemporary proposals for euthanasia and the Nazi programme. Maguire (1977) rebuts Alexander's assertion that 'it all started from small beginnings' together with his belief that if we allow any form of euthanasia we shall fall into the excesses of the Nazis. But he does not dismiss the Nazi analogy lightly: 'It did not happen', he says, 'in an ancient tribe centuries ago, but in a modern state with which we have not a few bonds of cultural kinship.' (Maguire, 1977, p. 321.) Yet he finds the analogy between the beginnings of the Nazi programme and contemporary proposals for euthanasia unacceptable. The substance of Maguire's objection to the analogy is to be found in his employment of a *retorqueo argumentum*, a form of argument which proceeds by turning the example back on the one who uses it. For these purposes Maguire offers three counter arguments to the use of the Nazi analogy in slippery slope objections to euthanasia.

(1) In the first argument, Maguire considers the early stages of the Nazi war machine which, like the euthanasia programme, started from 'small beginnings'. 'It began', says Maguire, 'when the first human beings began to kill one another to settle differences'. (Maguire, 1977, pp. 321–2.) Eventually it increased to the point of *Blitzkrieg* and the Nazi military atrocities of the Second World War. Consequently, to avoid the slope, we should conclude that all forms of killing, even those in self-defence, should be morally prohibited. 'If the Nazi analogy forbids euthanasia', argues Maguire, 'then it should also, and indeed *a fortiori*, given the history of military carnage, forbid war.' (Ibid., p. 322.)

The problem with Maguire's argument is that it is hard to see anything damaging to the slope argument in this analogy. The Nazi war machine provides a very good example of how far one can slide down a slope once it is accepted that war and killing people in order to settle differences is acceptable. This is why responsible peace-makers take every step to prevent the outbreak of war, since becoming like one's enemies is one of the dangers inherent in the adoption of their methods. One of the sad facts about the Second World War was the degree to which the Western democracies emulated the callousness of their enemies when they slid down the moral slope to Dresden and Hiroshima. Far from being a counter-example to the slope argument the Nazi war machine is a classic case of latent possibilities becoming actualities in a society which enthusiastically embraces the doctrine that war is an acceptable institution. There are very good grounds for restricting access to means of killing people, even if it means placing the onus of justification on those who are obliged to kill in self-defence. If Nero, Attila, or Phillip of Macedon, had had access to the industrial potential of the Rhine, there is every likelihood — since they accepted that war was a justifiable means of settling differences — that they would have gone as far down the slope as did Hitler.

(2) Maguire's second *retorqueo* argument is directed at those who see an analogy between contemporary proposals for sterilisation and the Nazi practice of eugenic sterilisation. Here his concern is with the suggestion that the Nazi programme of eugenic sterilisation 'might be argued as the basis for an absolutist stance against all forms of sterilisation'. (Maguire, 1977, p. 322.) But again it is hard to see how his rebuttal is damaging to the analogy. If it is desirable to avoid taking steps in the direction of the Nazi programme then it is necessary to campaign against all forms of involuntary sterilisation, and also to closely scrutinise each instance of voluntary sterilisation too. Maguire cites an example, reported in *Time* magazine, 23 July 1973, where children were sterilised without consent. If this is true then such behaviour warrants public condemnation and those responsible removed from office, lest they serve as the small beginnings which may establish a precedent for future abuses.

The strength of opposition to involuntary sterilisation was revealed in the case of a 17-year-old mentally-retarded girl who was sterilised following a ruling in favour by the Law Lords on 30 April 1987. The judgement and the debate around it brought to the foreground genuine fears of a wider programme of non-voluntary sterilisation. According to a leading article in the *Independent* the girl, a ward of court with a mental age of five, was not considered suitable for other forms of contraception because of 'her violent and aggressive behaviour, the likely interaction between contraceptive drugs and the anti-convulsants whch she receives for epilepsy, and the danger that her obesity and irregular periods might lead to a pregnancy being missed until it was too late for a safe abortion.' (*Independent*, 1 May 1987.) She was also considered likely to rip out an inter-uterine device if one were fitted and child-birth was considered to be 'too traumatic' for her and 'if a Caesarian were performed she would be likely to tear at the scar preventing it from healing.' (Ibid.)

Nevertheless, there was fierce opposition to the ruling and fears were expressed that it would open the floodgates to further sterilisations of mentally-handicapped minors. Sir Brian Rix, Secretary General of MENCAP, said in a joint statement with MIND, the National Association for Mental Health, that 'Sterilisation should only be undertaken when there are over-whelming medical reasons . . . In this case it appears that the circumstances approach the criteria but in our opinion do not fulfil them.' (Ibid.) Nevertheless, to stress that there should be no further steps towards widespread sterilisation the Law Lords insisted that their ruling should not be seen as a precedent and that all such sterilisations should in future be approved by a High Court judge. As a further precaution the Lord Chancellor, Lord Hailsham, emphasised that in this case the 'only consideration involved' was the 'well being, welfare or interests of the human being concerned', and that 'there was no issue of public policy other than the application of the above principle which could be taken into account, least of all any question of eugenics.' (Lord Hailsham, quoted by the *Independent*, 1 May 1987.)

Opposition to any form of eugenically motivated argument for sterilisation was also endorsed by another Law Lord, Lord Oliver, who emphasised that 'the case was not about sterilisation for social purposes; it was not about eugenics; it was not about the con-venience of those whose task it was to care for the ward or the anxieties of her family; and it involved no general principle of public policy.' (Lord Oliver, quoted by the *Independent*, 1 May 1987.)

Although the analogy with Nazi medical practices was not explicitly mentioned in this particular debate over sterilisation, it is nevertheless clear that an awareness of such a dangerous course lay behind the imperative to prevent unwarranted extension of involuntary sterilisation. On this occasion the assurances that no further extension was intended, and that the decision was taken in the interests of the patient, and that only a High Court judge could authorise further sterilisations, all indicated an awareness of just how precarious the sterilisation issue rests in relation to the slippery slope. Contemporary proposals for involuntary sterilisation are certainly not framed with reference to Nazi eugenics, but the fears of an extension of sterilisation into this area is still uppermost in the minds of serious moralists.

(3) Maguire's third argument is still harder to comprehend. He asks:

> Could not a case be constructed against the morality of developing and retaining nuclear weapons by citing the Hiroshima and Nagasaki atrocities? Such attacks could happen again. Development and deployment are not even 'small beginnings'. Therefore, if the thrust of the Nazi analogy used against death by choice is valid, all these should be considered, again *a fortiori*, as beyond the moral pale.' (Maguire, 1977, p. 322.)

The problem with Maguire's argument seems to be that far from serving as a counter-example to the slope argument, the Hiroshima-Nagasaki atrocities are generally considered to be well beyond the moral pale. Since 1945 serious people have argued, with considerable plausibility, that Hiroshima was the first step towards global destruction. Some 40 years after the event the extent of massive stockpiling of nuclear weapons indicates how near we are to it. There is no stronger example of the slippery slope prediction than the last four decades of nuclear weaponry.

It is when Maguire draws attention to specific differences between the Nazi programme and the modern euthanasia movement that his criticism of the analogy appears credible. His attempt to invalidate the analogy depends on the acceptance of four important differences between the two situations.

(1) The first point of difference is the different philosophical backgrounds out of which the respective euthanasia programmes emerged. According to Maguire 'the euthanasia programme of the Nazis was an explicit repudiation of the individualistic philosophy that animates this country'. (Maguire, 1977, p. 322.) Within the terms of the Nazi programme people were killed because they were considered as being of no use to the community. In contrast contemporary proponents of euthanasia advocate it only if it is beneficial to the individual. This is clearly an important distinction, but one which on closer examination is hard to maintain as a useful instrument of policy-making. Some individuals consider their lives to be useless to themselves if they are of little use to the community.

It would not be difficult to convince people that they no longer have any value to themselves once they are past their usefulness to the community. The high suicide rate among the involuntarily unemployed is a very strong reminder that an individual may see his or her life as useless because those responsible for determining the community's values have deemed that individual to be useless. If Maguire's distinction is to hold as a rebuttal of the Nazi analogy, we require yet more criteria to exlude those borderline cases from the programme. But it is the appeal to the inevitable problems of drawing up criteria of this sort that gives the slope argument its particular strength against Maguire's objections.

(2) Maguire sees a weakness in the Nazi analogy and claims that in the Germany of the 1930s there was a different social structure than in contemporary America. 'Our society', he says, 'is not nearly so homogenous as German society . . . our pluralism is incorrigible . . . There is no oneness . . . America is made up of unmeltable ethnics.' (Maguire, 1977, p. 323.) Fortunately there is a great deal of truth in this. But these remarks ignore certain pluralistic elements in pre-war Germany which was inhabited, not only by German-speaking people, but by Slavs, Jews, Gypsies, and no doubt many others whose existence the Nazis found incompatible with their racist objectives. Contemporary America, and the British Commonwealth too, consists of 'unmeltable ethnics', but many of these ethnic groups have been painfully aware that some Americans and British (usually WASPS) are considered to be more American and British than others. Contemporary society may be pluralistic but it is experienced as a hierarchic plurality. And it is this one aspect which engenders very real fears of a re-emergence of Nazism.

(3) Maguire's third objection to the Nazi analogy takes the form of an appeal to the Nazi experience itself. The reason why the Nazi analogy is invalid, he says, is because, unlike our predecessors, we have the Nazi experience as a warning of what might happen. 'The stark experiences of Nazism', says Maguire, 'have become important symbols in our collective conscience.' (Ibid.)

As a yardstick of what cannot be permitted the Nazi experience serves as a preventative against further steps down the slope; our knowledge about Nazism forewarns us against it. But even if we leave aside the standard objections about human failure to learn from history, Maguire's argument fails: on his own terms he cannot use this objection against the function of the Nazi analogy in the slippery slope argument; for his thesis is that the Nazi experience is irrelevant to contemporary moral issues. One cannot cite an appeal to the slippery slope of Nazism as a means of demonstrating the invalidity of such an appeal. If the Nazi experience has any relevance in contemporary moral deliberations it must be as a reminder of the worst that can happen. It is the awareness of the slope towards Nazism that serves as a preventative against adopting practices which point in that direction. The exponent of the slope argument cites them in order to prevent it happening again; it is therefore improper to cite them in order to demonstrate the redundancy of analogies with the Nazi experience. Maguire does not refute the slope argument with this example; he merely confirms it.

(4) Maguire's fourth objection to the Nazi analogy involves an appeal to the fact that the respective euthanasia proposals involve radically different contexts. In the contemporary debate on euthanasia death is being re-evaluated as a potential good, argues Maguire, 'not in an atmosphere where the utilitarian value of certain lives is the issue'. (Maguire, 1977, p. 323.) In the contemporary debate different questions determine the parameters of moral concern. 'The question currently is not whether life is worth living, but whether death, in its own good time, is worth dying.' (Ibid., p. 323.)

But is the context so different? Most arguments for euthanasia which insists that 'death is worth dying' are premised on the belief that the life in question is 'not worth living'. Living and dying are not two states, the benefits of which can be assessed independently; they are necessarily linked. Death is not a state in itself; it is the cancellation of life. If a culture comes to see death as a good which is preferable to life, it has simply devalued life by judging it not worth living. The difference between the life that is not worth living and the death that is worth dying is not sufficiently demonstrable to sustain a rejection of the Nazi analogy.

In order to sustain an acceptable rebuttal of the Nazi analogy one would need, as a minimum requirement, a genuine participatory democratic and pluralistic society within which the welfare of individual citizens is raised above theories and prejudices about alleged racial and ethnic supremacy, and where individual interests have priority over economic dogmas and theories of social utility. A few societies subscribe to these values, none show any signs of implementing them. Until they do the Nazi analogy is a reminder of an ever-present possibility.

The strength of the Nazi analogy in ethical debate is derived from the fact that in any culture, and within any field of human inquiry, there are certain references to major historical events which provide the yardsticks of appropriate conduct. In genetics there is the Lysenko episode; in discussions of the relationship between political control and technological development it is impossible to avoid references to the splitting of the atom and the Manhattan project. But no historical event has the world significance of the Nazi experience. Whether the topic is genetic engineering, *in vitro* fertilisation, prolongation of life, euthanasia, abortion, sterilisation, treatment of the mentally incompetent, experiments on humans, negative or positive eugenics, treatment of criminal or violent behaviour, or societal interest in reproductive patterns, the Nazi experience may be cited as a reference point. Often, references to this experience are made in a highly emotive manner. In so far as the Nazi analogy is invoked by exponents of the slope argument it is used to terminate discussion on certain proposals. This raises a very real danger of abusing the analogy, especially the risk of cheapening the moral currency of the events that took place in Nazi Germany. But instead of ruling out the analogy altogether it is more important to consider which kind of 'small beginnings' justify references to the Nazi experience and which do not. For example, the Nazi analogy is often employed against proponents of a more liberal attitude towards the voluntary termination of pregnancy. Yet current problems about abortion were not really aspects of the Nazi regime. In fact the Nazis discouraged abortion since their policy was to encourage the breeding of perfect Aryans. As for the alleged 'inferior' groups, abortion was never seen as an option since the 'racially impure' were subject to sterilisation.

The three most significant applications of the Nazi analogy in contemporary discussions focus on: eugenics and sterilisation; euthanasia; and experiments on human subjects. Only with an understanding of the meaning of these practices in Nazi Germany of yesterday and Western culture of today can one assess the ultimate value of the Nazi analogy and its relevance to the slippery slope argument.

Eugenics and sterilisation

From 1934 onwards all doctors in the German state apparatus were trained in racial biopolitics under Nazi party supervision.

Courses in *Rassenhygiene* (race-hygiene) were made compulsory for all medical personnel in various state institutions, including staff in psychiatric units. At the same time the general population were subjected to a continuous propaganda barrage about the need to protect the *Volk* by means of sterilisation of those deemed likely to jeopardise its purity. Now *Rassenhygiene* is not a concept which falls within the scope of contemporary medical practice, and methods deemed necessary to promote it are not analogous to practices like oral hygiene which are necessary for physical well-being. *Rassenhygiene* is an abstract concept, which under the Nazis was linked to even more abstract notions concerning the welfare of a race. The Nazi sterilisation programme was not based so much on a medical programme but rather on quasi-political concepts. Within medical practice one might promote a mass inoculation programme to protect the health of large groups of individuals from the threat of small-pox or diphtheria. But the promotion of programmes involving the sterilisation or destruction of 'valueless' lives was a response to an abstract notion.

In a discussion organised by the Hastings Center in 1976, on the relevance of the Nazi experience to today's problems, Dawidowicz (1976, pp. 3–4) maintained that since the Nazi programme was based on a theory of eugenics entailing beliefs in genetic purity there is no analogy between the Nazi case and the present range of ethical and social problems which confront us as a consequence of new developments in the life sciences. 'I do not think we can usefully apply the Nazi experience to gain insight or clarity to help us resolve our problems and dilemmas', she said. (1976, p. 3) '. . . What the Nazis meant by certain terms is not at all comparable to what we mean.' For Dawidowicz the very meaning of a term like 'sterilisation' is so fundamentally different in the Nazi case from its contemporary meaning that the analogy is disqualified: 'It's historically irrelevant to the contemporary debate.' (Ibid., p. 10.)

In formulating a reply to Dawidowicz it is important to concede, at the outset, that many of the issues in the contemporary debate on eugenics and sterilisation have little in common with Nazi theory. For the most part sterilisation is discussed today in a medical context with regard to hereditary diseases or family planning requirements. But it should also be noted that the line between medical and politico-social concepts is not absolutely clear in contemporary practice. Throughout Western thought, from Plato to contemporary political leaders, conceptual links have been drawn between medical science and biological notions of race. The notion of a healthy state and related veterinary concepts of stock-breeding were not the exclusive property of the Nazis. As long as metaphors derived from stock-breeding have a place in political discourse the Nazi analogy is a very important reminder of where they can lead if pursued with sufficient determinism. Volkish racism may not have much meaning in contemporary medicine, but it is all too familiar in contemporary culture to be ignored.

Notwithstanding certain fundamental differences between the Western democracies and the Third Reich, the thesis that the Nazi eugenics movement was a unique phenomenon, and that the concept of *Rassenhygiene* was confined to the Nazi episode, does not survive close scrutiny. In a study of the German eugenics programme during the nineteenth and twentieth centuries, Sheila Faith Weiss (1983) has argued with considerable plausibility that 'the understandable preoccupation of historians with the impact of racial and Aryan ideologies on Nazi political theory has obscured not only the context in which German eugenics developed . . . but also the legacy of the early movement for the later period'. (Weiss, 1983, p. 2.) Nazi race-hygiene, she argues is part of a broader intellectual and moral-political current in which medicine and science were seen to be allied to politics in an expression of a desire to improve the human race. This has sometimes reflected middle-class fears of the proletariat, anti-Semitism, or colour-prejudice, and has often been linked to various strands of Social Darwinism. But the end result is always the same: some groups are deemed 'degenerate' and 'unfit for survival', some lives are considered not 'worth living'.

According to Weiss, the German eugenics programme was part of a larger movement, whose origins share several similarities with the objectives of the Nazis. We can see this in the development of the concept of *Rassenhygiene* which, incidentally, has a broader scope than the English word 'eugenics', since it includes 'not only all attempts aimed at improving the hereditary quality of the population, but also measures directed towards an absolute increase in population'. (Weiss, 1983, p. 2.) *Rassenhygiene* was developed as a nineteenth-century doctrine by Willhelm Schallmayer (1857–1919) who saw it not so much as a racist objective but as a means of 'saving the economically and socially better-situated classes from biological extinction'. (Weiss, 1983, p. ii.) For Schallmayer, hereditary fitness was not to be assessed in terms of racist conceptions, but in 'terms of social productivity and social position',

(Weiss, 1983, p. ii), a view which reflected the fears and social prejudices of the educated middle classes of the late-nineteenth century.

Originally *Rassenhygiene* did not have the racist overtones that were later attached to it, but it nevertheless shared the same technocratic logic. Whereas the earlier movement expressed class interests the latter promoted a racist ideology, but both measured the worth of human beings by only two criteria; productivity and reproduction. In both cases the 'unfit' were the least productive citizens, such as homosexuals, alcoholics, criminals, the insane and feeble-minded, whose numbers from the late-nineteenth century onwards appeared to be rapidly growing.

There is little doubt that conceptual distinctions can be drawn between the nineteenth-century exponents of *Rassenhygiene* (like Schallmayer who saw race eugenics in terms of the promotion of hereditary fitness of all populations) and later eugenicists who subscribed to the Nordic ideal. These two formulations of eugenic policies were seen in the movement around the turn of the century. By 1905 the term *'Rasse hygiene'*, was overtaken by *Rassenhygiene* which was linked to the policies of racial supremacy. Although there was resistance in the early decades of the twentieth century, racist and Aryan enthusiasts within the eugenics movement managed to establish a strong foothold which later proved so dominant in the Nazi era. The history of the eugenics movement is a clear demonstration of how difficult it is to keep racists and supremacists out of a race-hygiene movement, whatever its objectives.

We can see this in the way that *Rassenhygiene* was attractive to members of the medical profession. Contrary to Dawidowicz, *Rassenhygiene* was not an aberration in German medical practice; it had been an integrated feature of the relationship between medicine and the state since the eighteenth century. According to Weiss:

> The medical profession's perception of themselves as the custodians of national health, and hence national wealth and efficiency — an important, if not the most important reason why so many physicians and hygienists embraced eugenics — has a long history. In Germany it dates back as early as the eighteenth century, when cameralist theorists and administrators enlisted the aid of physicians to help survey and regulate what most mercantile political thinkers agreed to

be the greatest source of national prosperity: a large and healthy workforce. All administrative measures designed to augment state power by ensuring the highest possible level of national health and vitality fell under the rubric of *medizinische Polizei* (medical police) — a concept which includes such practices as the computation of statistics on disease, life expectancy, and fertility and mortality rates, as well as rudimentary public health programmes. (Weiss, 1983, pp. 31–3.)

The term *medizinische Polizei*, which is indicative of a close relationship between medicine and the objectives of the civil authorities, was first employed by a German physician Wolfgang Thomas Rau in 1764, who held that the medical profession 'not only has an obligation to treat the sick, but also to oversee the health of the entire population'. (Cited by Weiss, 1983, p. 33.)

Although it must be conceded that the initial objective of the *Rassenhygiene* programme was not committed to Volkish racism there are sufficient overlaps which suggest that the Nazi eugenics movement did not spring like Athena from the head of Zeus, and that steps from the early eugenics movement to the Nazi programme were gradual once the central presuppositions were accepted. These consisted of the following beliefs.

(1) *The belief that the medical profession were the guardians of the nation's health and prosperity.* This belief grew against a background of nineteenth- and early twentieth-century successes in scientific medicine, successes in bacteriology, and preventative medicine. Throughout this period the German medical profession, including psychiatrists, were trained in the hereditarian tradition. Accordingly, sterilisation of mentally-defective individuals was not such a radical step. Add to this some of the racist creeds of the twentieth century and we have a fertile ground for the Nazi programme.

(2) *The belief that Slavonic and Asian races constituted a threat to European interests.* Given the fact that an important feature of the race-hygiene movement was the stimulation of population growth, the awareness of Germany's falling birthrate before the First World War could easily be presented in terms of an 'advantage' for the Asians and Slavs. Of significance here is the perceived threat from Japan after its military victory over the Russians in 1905.

(3) *The cult of motherhood.* The rise of feminism and the birth-control movement around the turn of the century, which was largely a middle-class phenomenon, produced fears of a declining

middle-class overtaken by the proletariat. As a reaction many eugenicists embraced various motherhood cults. This doctrine was later promoted by the Nazis and became a powerful form of the oppression of women during the Third Reich. Illegal termination of pregnancy was made a capital offence and access to contraception and birth-control devices were restricted. But women who had faithfully served the Reich, by producing at least four healthy children, were eligible for the 'Iron Cross of German Motherhood'. When Gerhard Wagner, leader of the National Socialist's 'Doctors' Association' declared that 'the nation's stock of ovaries are a natural resource, and property of the state', he only reiterated in a harsher tone Schallmayer's own views on the subject: women's bodies were manipulated goods which 'must be managed in the interests of the state.' (Weiss, 1983, pp. 315–16.)

(4) *Fiscal criteria for the evaluation of human beings.* The fourth factor common to both earlier and later stages of the eugenics movement is also suggestive of contemporary analogies with Nazism. It is the reduction of complex value problems to over simplified economic objectives. Despite claims about the guardianship of the nation's health the excesses of Nazi eugenics were primarily motivated by economic concerns. According to Weiss:

> Although euthanasia had been discussed in legal and medical circles long before Hitler seized power, it was only under the financial strains of war that plans were actually undertaken to clear out Germany's psychiatric institutions of 'lives not worth living'. The real motivation, all attempts to pass the killings off as humanitarian notwithstanding, was economic. Long regarded by Schallmayer and other Wilhelmine and Weimar eugenicists as both unproductive and costly, the insane were viewed by the Nazis as 'lives devoid of all value' — lives unworthy of any government expense. (Weiss, 1938, p. 313.)

Although the Nazis went much further down the slope than the earlier eugenicists their logic, argues Weiss, was determined by the same objectives: 'the rational management of national efficiency'. (Weiss, 1983, p. 314.)

These four sets of beliefs, which were held in common between exponents of earlier and later eugenics, are widely held today. The alliance of medicine and science, in the interests of the state;

perceived threats from non-Europeans; reaction against feminism and an intrusion of cost-benefit criteria in health care decision-making has decidedly modern aspects.

Other conceptual parallels between Nazi theories of 'health' and contemporary beliefs have been noted. One of the contributors to the Hastings Center discussion on the relevance of the Nazi analogy, Joseph Walsh, noted cultural similarities between the Nazis and the contemporary 'leftist' counter-culture in science. Looking through the documents of the pre-Nazi era, Walsh noted that:

> There is a real rebirth of the notion of wholeness, unity with the universe, the critiques of the excessive objectivity of science, of the need for the medical profession in particular to address itself to the whole man and not to be concerned only with particular diseases. From what I've seen (and I don't know how representative this is), these kinds of intellectual currents were present under the umbrella of the Nazi movement. (Walsh, 1976, p. 11.)

Perhaps this aspect of the analogy should not be pushed too far, but it is not hard to see how a fixation with wholeness can have a bearing on the belief that a whole world would be better off without certain members who were less than whole. Within these terms a sterilisation and euthanasia programme, aimed at the health of the gene pool, is not that unthinkable today.

Euthanasia

According to Dawidowicz, the meaning of the term 'euthanasia' is not the same in Nazi literature as it is in current usage. It was a code name, she says, 'which the Nazis used as both camouflage and euphemism for a programme of murder — killing various categories of persons because they were regarded as racially "valueless, deformed, insane, senile or any combination thereof". ' (Dawidowicz, 1976, p. 3.) The Nazi euthanasia programme functioned in two areas: the killing of deformed children, which was carried out on an individual basis; and the killing of the adult insane and other diseased states within the categories deemed appropriate for euthanasia. This undertaking gave the Nazis their first experience of mass killing. But according to Dawidowicz, in neither area was the killing analogous to current proposals for euthanasia. Killing was never administered because of a 'sick or dying person's intolerable suffering or because of a patient's own feelings about the uselessness of his life'. (Ibid., p. 4.) Says Dawidowicz:

> In no case did the patient ask for death. Killing was done without the patient's consent and — except for that first case — without the family's knowledge. In fact, the notifications of death that the medical-killing stations sent to the families concealed the actual manner of death. Families were informed that their kin had died of pneumonia or during an appendectomy. (The lie was detected in instances when the family knew that the patient's appendix had been removed many years earlier.) (Ibid., p. 4.)

The Nazi euthanasia programme, argues Dawidowicz, does not have the same rationale as contemporary proposals for euthanasia. The killing took place in the wider context of a racially motivated genocidal strategy. As well as the medical programme, the Nazis had plans for killing Jews, Russians, Communists and trade unionists.

In a recent proposal for euthanasia in the case of grossly deformed infants, Kuhse and Singer (1985) cite Dawidowicz's distinction between the Nazi euthanasia programme and contemporary proposals, arguing that Leo Alexander

> . . . has badly misunderstood the Nazi terminology. The misunderstanding vitiates his attempt to use the historical experience of Nazism as an argument against euthanasia as we now understand the term. When the Nazis talked of 'a life not worthy to be lived' they meant that life was unworthy because it did not contribute to the health of that mysterious racial entity, the *Volk*. Since our society does not believe in any such entity, there is no real prospect that allowing active euthanasia of severely mentally handicapped new-born infants would lead to Nazi-style atrocities. (Kuhse and Singer, 1985, p. 95.)

An immediate reaction to Kuhse and Singer here is that racism in our culture is very much alive and that the homogeneity presupposed by the expression 'our society' simply does not exist.

However, it may be the case that despite the existence of racism in Western society, contemporary medicine does not have notions of the 'Volk' at its core. But there is an increasing concern with social utility which may turn out to be not that far removed from the Nazi standpoint. In Hitler's Germany, Volkish racism often went hand-in-hand with notions of social utility. Hitler condemned the 'non-rehabitable' as 'useless eaters'. He might have been obsessed with racist notions, but his idea of killing them because they were too expensive to maintain was part of the same argument. For Hitler, racism and social utility were not incompatible. Though analytically separable these notions are easily harmonised. One can add a racist flavour to 'socially useless'. Certain races may be deemed useless, and hence harmful to the Volk.

This point was noted by another contributor to the Hastings Center discussion, Laurence McCullogh, who, whilst recognising the weakness of the analogy with Nazi racism in some respects, saw an analogy between some contemporary values and the Nazi concept of social utility. McCullogh conceded that the Nazis started on the slippery slope because of their racist ideology but he also saw certain aspects of the analogy which might hold today:

> Of course the two situations may simply be too far removed, and so the analogy loses its force. We see that what got German society on the slippery slope, indeed what characterized the slope, was the racist attitudes already in place. It is a reasonable defence and distinguishes our case from theirs, for us to say that we don't have those attitudes. (McCullogh, 1976, p. 15.)

Nevertheless, McCullogh adds a crucial qualification:

> That is not a complete answer, however. We have to be careful about what aspects of our society we focus on. *Our* slippery slope might yet be analogous to Germany's in a more abstract way. If we consider the rationale which gives social utility or economic returns precedence over individual freedom, then we might see how our society could approach the kind of thinking that underlay the Nazi experience. There, racism overrode personal autonomy; here, it might be an economic rationale — the attitude that we won't spend so much per year to keep somebody alive on the slim chance of recovery.

29

The slippery slope then is not the participating act; its the context in which the act takes place. The Nazi slope was one of racism; in the United States . . . what we have is an economic calculus which would, so one would have to argue, be the analogue of Nazi racism in sacrificing individual freedom to the interests of others. (McCullogh, 1976, p. 15.)

The point behind McCullogh's remarks is that if there is a point in drawing an analogy between the Nazi experience and today one needs to understand what beliefs are held in common. For the Nazis it was a dubious theory of racial purity which led them down the slope; today the slope may begin with the employment of cost-benefit criteria for the evaluation of a life. But in both cases the common factor is that, for whatever grounds, some lives are deemed not to be worth living. It is that attitude, as Leo Alexander warned after the Nuremberg trials, which indicates the first step on the slope.

Experiments on human subjects

The record of Nazi experiments on human beings is one of the most horrific incidents in human history. But it is not an isolated aberration associated exclusively with the Third Reich. As details emerge about Japanese experiments on prisoners during the Second World War it becomes clear that the propensity to inflict harm on innocent human beings was not peculiar to the Nazis.

There can be no moral defence of Nazi research on human beings. In the interests of research the Nazis shot Russian prisoners-of-war through the spleen to measure rates of bleeding; human beings were dissected under water to examine the effects of explosive decompression; people were systematically frozen to death to test treatments for exposure; diets of unaltered sea water were tested on groups of gypsies; the use of sulfonamides against gangrene was tested by deliberately creating wounds and infecting them. A professor of anatomy at the University of Strasbourg had 150 Jews murdered so that their skeletons could be preserved against the expected extinction of their group. (Dougherty, 1985, p. 8.)

Fortunately there is nothing as grotesque in contemporary medical research, although the situation with regard to experiments on human beings at present is far from satisfactory. In a paper which argues for clearly defined criteria for permissible experiments on human beings, Dougherty (1985) cites numerous contemporary practices which serve as a warning that a willingness to impose risk on some persons for the benefit of others was not strictly confined to medical research in Nazi Germany. According to Dougherty 'to test whether or not urethal reflux can occur in normal bladders, vesicoure-thrography was carried out on 26 normal babies less than forty-eight hours old. These infants were exposed to X-rays while their bladders were filling and voiding.' (Dougherty, 1985, p. 6.) In some cases children seeking various therapies have been used as unsuspecting guinea-pigs. 'Of 130 children being studied to record the effect of hyposensitisation therapy for bronchial asthma, 91 received therapeutically inert injections of buffered saline for periods of up to fourteen years without the knowledge of either child or parent.' (Ibid.)

Although information on and disclosure about research and experiments conducted on prisoners in the United Kingdom is hampered by the Official Secrets Act, there is evidence from American prisons that prisoners are often subjected to dubious experiments. Dougherty records prisoners in Oregon who were 'submitted to repeated bilateral testicular biopsies and injections of radioactive thymidine to test the rate of spermatogenesis.' (Ibid.) In California:

> . . . extreme 'acting out' criminal offenders were involved in aversive conditioning experiments with a drug which creates muscular paralysis and sensations of suffocation. Five of these prisoners later claimed that they had been forced against their wills and eighteen reported that they had felt pressured to participate. Eleven prisoners in Iowa submitted to experimentally induced scurvy and produced swollen and bleeding gums, perifollicular hemorrhages, joint swelling and pain, conjuntival hemorrhages, and bilateral femoral neuropathy. (Dougherty, 1985, pp. 6–7.)

None of these experiments produced anything that was not known before. In fact most of the results had been known for centuries.

The mentally-handicapped have been frequently exploited in the service of research. In one widely-reported study of the infectiousness of hepatitis, researchers at an American institution for mentally-handicapped children artificially induced hepatitis in the children. In some cases the parents objected but later co-operated when it was pointed out that the continuance of care in the institution would be withdrawn if they refused to co-operate. (Dougherty, 1985, p. 7; see also Ramsey, 1970, pp. 53–4.)

Another example of 'enforced voluntarisation' occurred in a mental hospital in Vietnam where an American psychiatrist tested aversive conditioning on Vietnamese schizophrenics. They were given a choice between unmodified electroconvulsion treatment or volunteering themselves for a work programme. Those who accepted treatment and still refused work were denied food for three days until they volunteered for work. (Dougherty, 1985, p. 7.)

Apart from these examples, where patients are pressured to participate in ethically dubious experiments, there are occasions when patients have unknowingly participated in risky experiments. In 1982 Diana Melrose published her study of the misapplication of health care in underdeveloped countries. This revealed the extent to which experimental drugs are distributed without adequate information to consumers in the poorer countries. (Melrose, 1982.) A similar disregard of the genuine needs of the sick has been displayed *within* the Western democracies. In Dougherty's survey one American experiment 'to determine portal circulation time and hepatic blood flow involved transcutaneous injection of the spleen and cathetisation of the hepatic vein'. (Dougherty, 1985, p. 7.) This was carried out on 43 subjects. Published reports made no mention of the estimations regarding the risks involved, which were considerable as 29 subjects involved were 'already suffering from cirrhosis, acute hepatitis, and hemolytic anaemia.' (Ibid.)

Perhaps one of the more emotionally charged cases was the widely-reported experiment in New York during July 1963, where '22 seriously ailing and debilitated inhabitants of a relatively obscure Brooklyn institution, the Jewish Chronic Disease Hospital', were injected with live cancer cells. (Langer, 1983, p. 629.) Although the circumstances under which these patients consented to these proceedings was ambiguous further investigation indicated that 'some of these patients were in such a physical and mental condition that they were incapable of understanding the nature of this experiment or giving an informed consent thereto.' (Ibid., p. 632.)

It might be objected that the analogy between Nazi experiments on human beings and contemporary experiments breaks down on the grounds that the former were non-voluntary whilst in the latter the subjects were volunteers. However, the concept of 'enforced voluntarisation' obscures this distinction. Some 'volunteers' may be motivated by extreme poverty. Thus for two dollars an hour subjects in one American experiment had their reactions to LSD tested, although no mention was made at the time of the possible adverse effects on their personalities. Most cases of enforced voluntarisation involve the participation of the poorest and most desperate sections of society. Says Dougherty:

> Although solid evidence was already available as to its effectiveness as a treatment of typhoid fever, choloramphenicol was witheld from 157 of 408 charity patients with typhoid fever. The death rate of the choloramphenicol treated group was 7.97 per cent; of those receiving no choloramphenicol, 22.9 per cent. This means that (approximately) 23 persons died to confirm that already well-confirmed result. (Dougherty, 1985, p. 7.)

These cases are clearly disturbing, although they do not match the horror and scale of the Nazi atrocities. Nor were they connected with a unified programme of extermination guided by conceptions of Volkish racism. But in a limited sense an analogy holds in that those put at risk for the alleged benefits of others are drawn from sections of society already held in low esteem, such as ethnic minorities, criminals, the poor, and the insane.

It may be argued that it is only with reference to possible abuses to living subjects that a limited analogy with Nazi experimental practices is relevant. Experiments upon cadavers and the harvesting of vital organs of the recently deceased all have obvious beneficial possibilities without any potential harm for the ex-patient. So great is the demand for organ transplants that several ethicists have proposed that the consent of the donor should be waived; that the duty to a living patient should outweigh a person's reluctance to posthumously donate organs, and that, providing there are no proposals for compulsory live organ donation, there should be a presumption in favour of donation. (Harris, 1985.)

This proposal, however, runs counter to what many consider to be a basic right; that individuals have a right to decide what shall be done with their bodies. Now Harris recognises this right, and even extends it to cover what he sees as the right to assisted suicide. There would seem to be no reason, on these grounds, for diminishing such rights when they apply to the disposal of one's remains any more than the right to bequeath organs after one's death should be restricted.

There is, moreover, a slippery slope objection to proposals for compulsory organ donation. It turns on the issue as to which agency should have the authority to extract organs in such cases. Should the state have the power to override the individual's known wishes or should this authority be given to some other agency? But even if it were the latter it would only do so under some kind of licence or delegated authority from the state; in which case the end result would be a significant increase in the state's control over an individual's body. The issue then becomes one of a choice between either a genuine desire to save lives by increasing the number of organ donors, or increasing the powers of the state. Now it may be that an enhancement of the state's power is quite an acceptable price to pay for the number of lives saved through compulsory harvesting of organs. But the significance of the slope argument here is in its ability to focus attention on the fact that greater state involvement is a necessary consequence of the proposal which, for many, is a step that should not be taken too hastily. The spectre of a state department with absolute rights over our remains, and those of our loved ones, is reminiscent of totalitarianism. Furthermore, given the fact that few states, despite their democratic protestations, place an equal value on all sections of the community, there is the added fear that in some cases the state may have an interest in accelerating the dying process. Such may be this fear, that many of the less privileged members of the community would have genuine fears of surgery lest they end up as premature organ donors. A state with the power to dispose as it sees fit with the deceased's organs might not be that far removed from one which made similar dispositions prior to the death of its least valued members. So, on further examination, it may turn out that fear of greater state involvement, generated by the slope argument, may provoke people into thinking about alternative methods of increasing the number of available transplant organs, such as a more effective and informative campaign for voluntary donors.

Could it happen here?

It is often said that the Nazi slide from the legalisation of euthanasia to the death camps must be understood as an aspect of a totalitarian society. On these terms the analogy with Nazi Germany is only valid if current proposals for euthanasia are advanced in the context of a totalitarian regime. In a pluralistic society, so the argument goes, the medical profession, the churches, and other groups, are capable of organising resistance to proposals which could lead to the excesses experienced under totalitarian regimes. There were, of course, notable protests against the Nazi euthanasia programme between 1939 and 1941 when the families of some of the victims realised what was going on. Protests were made through the churches and some bishops — such as Bishop Galen of Munster — expressed Catholic opposition. But it is very significant that the medical profession did not resist.

One reason for this, as we have seen, was the acceptance of quasi-political concepts as an intrinsic aspect of medical practice and research. But for those who dissented, fear was an important factor. Telford Taylor explains how many German doctors avoided a dangerous confrontation of the ethical values with the exponents of Nazi medical practices. He cites an expression, used at that time, which referred to a 'flight into the army'. (Taylor, 1976.) By joining the army one could be a patriotic German and still fight against the enemy without being confronted by the difficult problems back home. On these terms one avoided exposing one's ethical objections to methods of defending the Volk against alleged racial impurity by enlisting for the Eastern front to protect it from the alleged Russian threat. This was seen as one way out.

Other reasons are equally related to the totalitarian nature of Nazi Germany in that those who had deep ethical objections against what they were required to do also experienced feelings of hopelessness, and saw protest as futile. One German surgeon, under the pseudonym, Peter Bann, wrote about the extermination of Jews:

A few months later the 11th Army captured Sevastopol, whereupon all the Jewish inhabitants were collected and put to death in special poison vans. We knew all this, yet we did nothing. If anyone had protested or undertaken some positive action against the murder squad, he would have been arrested twenty-four hours later and would have disappeared. It is one of the most inglorious strategies of the totalitarian system

35

that they gave their opponents no opportunity to die a martyr's death for their convictions. For this there would have been no shortage of candidates. But a man who chooses this death, rather than the silent toleration of such atrocities, would have sacrificed his life in vain. I do not of course imply that such self-sacrifice would have been useless in a moral sense. I am only saying that as a practical measure it would have been pointless. (Cited by Taylor, 1976, p. 12.)

There is little doubt that the very totalitarian nature of Nazi society was a crucial factor in the slope from euthanasia to other forms of inflicting harm on human beings. But totalitarian regimes do not emerge from nowhere; they usually have a set of values which are shared by a significant number of people. In Nazi Germany it was Volkish racism and anti-Semitism together with a willingness to accept a principle of social utility, that some lives were not worth living. So if there is any merit in citing the parade of Nazi atrocities it must be because those tendencies, however small, are present today.

At the Nuremberg trials after the Second World War it was established that obedience by a soldier to command resulting in an unlawful act should be considered a crime. The excuse, 'I was only obeying orders', was no longer considered acceptable. During the 1960s and early 1970s several studies were undertaken to evaluate the extent to which persons would (under carefully defined circumstances involving obedience to authority) be willing to inflict harm on others. One of the widely discussed studies of this period was the Milgram experiments (Milgram, 1974) which investigated the conditions under which a cross-section of the population can be induced to inflict pain and danger to other people. These experiments focused on the *behavioural* responses of subjects in a situation of psychological conflict. Several 'volunteers' were given the impression that they were inflicting pain on unseen victims by administering increasingly lethal does of electric shocks to subjects who were making mistakes in a learning experiment. At a certain level of 'pain' the volunteers heard the victims cry out, beat on the walls, and plead for the experiment to be stopped. At this point, when the volunteers had turned to the experimenter for advice, they were told to carry on. Out of the 40 participants, 26 went on to administer the highest shock on the generator. Although no pain was actually inflicted and the cries of pain were pre-recorded, this was not known by the volunteers who believed that they were administering electric shocks to the other person. The conclusion from this experiment was that, despite the Nuremberg ruling that blind obedience is not an excuse for wrongdoing, the Milgram subjects revealed a willingness to carry out what are commonly regarded as obviously immoral and possibly illegal actions. Moreover, their compliance was even more surprising given the fact that the usual wartime propaganda about the iniquities of the enemy was missing. In this case the only incentive was the authority relationship between experimenter and subject. Despite serious reservations concerning the ethics of placing the subjects under such levels of nervous tension it was accepted that, given the appropriate circumstances, the human capacity to inflict harm has not diminished, nor was it confined to the Nazi era.

It may be objected that a willingness to inflict harm at the behest of an authority is still a long way from the acceptance of doctrines committed to a Nazi 'final solution'. The conclusion of the Milgram experiments certainly provided a partial explanation of harm done to others in certain political contexts. Yet obedience itself is not a sufficient explanatory concept for the behaviour we associate with a willingness to tolerate harm done to others. An examination of current attitudes towards harm inflicted on others where no authoritarian pressures are evident may indicate the extent to which Nazi theories about the 'final solution' would be accepted today.

There is overwhelming evidence that violence and tolerance of aggression together with the approval of the use of force as a legitimate political instrument are part of our cultural values. The popular support for the employment of violence as a legitimate political means can be seen in the enthusiastic response to the Falklands War among the British public, although it might be doubted that the reaction of one of Britain's mass-circulation newspapers, the *Sun*, whose notorious headline 'Gotcha', after the sinking of the Argentinian cruiser, *Belgrano*, accurately reflected the consensus of British opinion. The same could be said for that newspaper's headline, 'Thrilled to Blitz' following the British supported bombing raid made by the Americans on Libya in 1986. Against a background of the popular media endorsing violence and jingoism one must really sympathise with British soccer hooligans whose disappointment over lack of recognition for their 'patriotism' is felt deeply. (When one British participant in a soccer riot in Amsterdam in 1986 was quoted in several national newspapers as saying: 'Brilliant. We did our bit for English football', he was, perhaps, accurately reflecting the values of those very newspapers who were critical of him.)

The widespread toleration of violence affects our attitudes towards aggression and the victims of aggression. There are frequent complaints of the unsympathetic attitudes towards victims of sexual assault and there is no political mileage in campaigns on behalf of the victims of police assault. Recent studies of domestic violence stress that it is more widespread than hitherto suspected, and researchers in this subject area have frequently commented on the reluctance of law enforcement agencies to effectively combat it. (See Brophy and Smart, 1985.)

Perhaps the most dramatic examples of tolerance to harm can be seen in what has been described as 'The innocent bystander' phenomenon, where spectators to an act of aggression make no effort to help the victim. In 1964 Americans were shocked when they read in their newspapers that Kitty Genovese was murdered in front of 38 people, none of whom came to her help or alerted the police. Since then cases of this kind have become commonplace. Yet none of them come under the explanatory concept of obedience. Indeed, there is often a hostility to the victims which seems to reinforce a crude Social Darwinism, whereby the fit survive and the unfit victims of aggression 'deserve' to perish.

Other means by which a tolerance for violence is reflected in Western culture can be described in terms of a 'Don't want to know' syndrome. White South Africans who visit Europe often exhibit surprise at the world-wide concern about the violence in their culture — they themselves have simply ignored it. Similarities can be seen in the way in which the British public remain in a state of moral apathy towards the violence of Northern Ireland, which receives more attention by foreign observers. The very closeness of violence can sometimes immunise one's sensitivity to it.

These forms of tacit acceptance of violence should not be underrated when one is assessing the overall tolerance of violence in a culture.

To assess the willingness to participate in, or endorse, a programme of killing, Helge Hilding Mansson carried out an investigation into the condition that affect people's attitudes towards killing. The initial hypothesis guiding the research was that 'social distance' (i.e. the degree of non-identification with and degree of perceived threat by certain groups) would increase the respondent's willingness to endorse their killing as a 'final solution', as long as the final solution was carried out 'objectively' and 'scientifically'. (Mansson, 1977, p. 309.) For the purpose of the study the perceived threat was from the mentally and emotionally 'unfit', minority groups in the USA, and the Asian population. The results were published under the ironic title, 'Justifying the Final Solution'.

Mansson's survey was addressed to middle-class Americans of reasonable educational levels. The subjects consisted of part-time university students in the 17 to 48 age group. They were told that 'education and birth-control devices are not succeeding in controlling the population explosion' and that 'new measures are being considered by several of the major powers of the world including our own'. (Mansson, 1977, p. 310.) It was explained to the subjects that the 'new measures' involved 'mercy killing', which, they were told, was considered by most experts as being 'not only beneficial to the unfit', but 'more importantly it will be beneficial to the healthy, fit, and more educated segment of the population'. (Ibid., p. 310.) They were also told that these 'new measures' of mercy killing would be a 'final solution to a grave problem', and that the only remaining problems were those of devising which methods of killing should be employed, who should do the killing, and who should decide when it should be done. The subjects were asked to participate in means of solving these problems and told that as soon as the system was perfected it would be applied to humans. (Ibid., p. 310.) Out of the 570 participants, 326 approved and 244 disapproved of the 'final solution'.

Unlike the Milgram experiments, where the subjects were placed in a coercive setting, the social setting governing Mansson's research 'was such that the respondents could express their beliefs without being coerced'. (Mansson, 1977, p. 316.) Mansson stressed that throughout the experiment decisions were anonymous and freely arrived at in the 'absence of any obedience to command'. (Ibid., p. 317.) The perception that the 'final solution' was worthwhile (i.e. putting the unfit 'out of their misery'), probably influenced their decision, and the fact that *they* had been asked for assistance was flattering, thus enhancing a tendency to agree with the experimenters. Taking these factors into consideration it is hard to disagree with Mansson's overall conclusion that, 'the values ordinarily associated with a commitment to, and a belief in, the sacredness or worthwhileness of human life are not unqualifiedly shared by everyone'. (Ibid., p. 316.) The thoroughness of the opinion sample suggests that a Nazi euthanasia programme would find widespread acceptance among educated sections in the Western democracies. Says Mansson: 'The strength and intensity with which the subjects stuck to their justifications were real. And so were their beliefs that mass killings can be justified.' (Ibid., p. 318.)

3

The Sanctity of Life

Many arguments proclaiming the sanctity of life are premised on the belief in a Creator of life together with the belief that life is a gift which this benevolent being has bestowed upon the living. Accordingly, one's attitudes towards life might be determined by beliefs concerning the status of the Creator.

In some formulations of the sanctity of life principle all forms of life are considered morally valuable. In other formulations human life is singled out as having an exclusive moral value, since the Creator, it is alleged, fashioned human beings in His own image. This has raised problems among some supporters of the sanctity of life principle, especially regarding the extent of their moral obligations to non-human animals. Should moral concern over non-humans be based on the possession of certain characteristics associated with human beings, such as cognition? If so, how can cognition be assessed? No doubt this question deserves lengthy discussion for it is related to fundamental philosophical issues regarding the essence of humanity and the relationship between human beings and their environment. However, for the purpose of this discussion, the moral *aspects* of cognition will not be given ultimate priority over other aspects of life. The introduction of cognition as a qualifying condition for moral respect would be a step towards the exclusion of a wide range of beings who, according to moral consensus in civilised societies, are recognised as members of a moral community. These would include human beings in persistent vegetative states, anencephalic infants, foetuses, and many non-human animals. Moreover, since cognition is an indeterminate concept there are inevitable borderline problems with potential for slippery slopes. Where, it might be asked, is a line to be drawn according to which higher primates, dolphins, or severely mentally damaged human beings, could be classified as either cognitive or non-cognitive beings? But whether or not these beings are treated as members of a moral community is an issue that is usually settled before discussions about cognition begin.

In much of Christian theology the wrongness of taking life is bound up with the wrongness of mishandling what ultimately belongs to the Creator. In so far as Christian teachings have had a profound influence on Western medicine the thesis that life is a divine gift is part of the slippery slope objections to various proposals for accelerated death. Any liberalisation of the laws which currently prohibit euthanasia, so the argument goes, would be the first step on a slope which begins with the departure from the sanctity of life principle and ends with the toleration of various inhuman forms of killing. But the problem is that, for the deist, the slope actually begins, not with the liberalisation of rules prohibiting euthanasia, but when questions are posed regarding the authenticity of the Creator. In a secular age, so it would seem, the crucial steps down the slippery slope have already been taken. It would seem that shorn of its theological infrastructure the sanctity of life argument is an inadequate brake for the slippery slope.

One proposed solution is to replace the theologically grounded 'sanctity-of-life ethic by a quality-of-life approach'. (Kuhse, 1982, p. 33.) The reasons for this move are that, in a secular age, the sanctity of life ethic 'is no longer able to guide our actions in an unequivocal way'. (Ibid., p. 33.) There is some truth in this approach for the theological ramifications of the sanctity of life argument seem far removed from the context in which contemporary problems in the biomedical sciences arise. The problem is that quality of life concepts fall into that category of undetermined concepts which are even less likely to provide an unequivocal guide for our actions.

Although the slope argument is an integral feature of the sanctity of life principle it need not stand or fall with the theological assumptions underpinning the sanctity of life argument. But if the slope argument is to have any validity in a secular age, then arguments regarding the moral status of life must be shown to be independent of arguments about the nature and function of a Creator of life. If life is good it cannot be sufficient to say that it is good because it is a gift. Some gifts are not worth keeping, and some have too many strings attached to them.

Utilitarian and consequentialist doctrines are of little use when formulating alternatives to the sanctity of life principle. With sufficient imagination one can easily produce innumerable utilitarian or consequentialist arguments in favour of taking lives. Conversely, utilitarian and consequentialist doctrines are of little value when trying to establish the wrongness of killing. One might, for example, argue for the wrongness of killing by means of an appeal to certain consequences, such as the sorrow of relatives or the horror suffered by witnesses. But the problem with appeals to utilitarian 'side-effects' of this kind is that, under appropriate circumstances, they can always be eliminated thus leaving the belief in the wrongness of killing without any support.

A better course is to replace the sanctity of life principle, and all of its theological ramifications, with a principle concerning the 'value of life', expressed in the statement that 'life is worth living'. The reason why it is wrong to kill is that life is worth living. This applies to humans and non-humans and corresponds with a commonsense intution shared by most decent people, that non-humans are morally significant. There is no problem in finding reasons for this belief; the problem is merely that of excluding some of the more trivial reasons. Every experience can be a reason for living. Sensory experiences, like eyesight, hearing and so on are part of life and are worth having in the sense that we consider those deprived of them as being handicapped. The same can be said for mental experiences, emotions and so forth. Life, which furnishes any being with these goods, is worth living.

It may be objected that the faculties for experience, such as perceptions, desires, activities and thoughts, can be vehicles of both pleasant and unpleasant experiences and that should the bad experiences outweigh the good then life would not be worth living. Thomas Nagel meets this objection when he argues that 'even if one is undergoing terrible experiences' (Nagel, 1979, p. 2) it is good to be alive:

> There are elements which, if added to one's experience, make life better; there are other elements which, if added to one's experience, make life worse. But what remains when these are set aside is not merely *neutral*: it is emphatically positive. Therefore life is worth living even when the bad elements of experience are plentiful, and the good ones too meager to outweigh the bad ones on their own. The additional positive weight is supplied by experience itself, rather than by any of its contents. (Nagel, 1979, p. 2.)

There are three important characteristics of the value of life principle which can be retained in the principle that 'life is worth living'. First, if the principle that life is worth living has any value at all it must be meant in an absolute sense. That is to say, there can be no watering down of the principle to accommodate situations where killing is recognised to be justifiable. It is important to recognise that circumstances where killing may be justified (such as killing in self-defence) are not, in themselves, breaches of the principle that 'life is worth living', and consequently do not call for any reformulation of the principle in order to admit them. Second, as an absolute principle its function is to provide moral justification for actions, although it does not require justification itself. Third, if it does not require justification then it is not accepted as a matter of choice. If we put ourselves in a position of trying to invent the moral rules for a community, then it would be hard to avoid drawing the following conclusions reached by Robert Veatch:

> Either life really is not sacred (that is, it really can be violated) or life is sacred and real-world behaviour does not conform to what morality requires. I find myself pressured towards the second option; that is, when I try to put myself in the position of attempting to invent the moral rules for the community, and especially when I place myself in the position of one attempting to discern the rules, I find that the prohibition on killing is one that I must cling to. It is morally an ultimate, and, therefore, no reason can be given for the conclusion any more than one can give reasons for choosing the principles of beneficence, liberty, veracity, or contract keeping. It is the very nature of a fundamental principle that no reasons can be given to explain it. If they could be, then the principle would not be truly fundamental in this ultimate sense. If that position can be maintained regarding the principle of avoiding killing (although most people seem to think it cannot), then the prohibition on active killing for mercy is easy to understand. If all killings are prohibited simply because the taking of life is fundamentally outside of human discretion, then taking of life for mercy must be prohibited as well. According to this view, it is not a matter of the bad consequences, though these may be bad enough. The prohibition is even more basic. (Veatch, 1984, p. 233.)

In medicine the prohibition against the taking of life is not so much a consequence of accepting certain principles; it is much more basic and is bound up with the very nature of medicine. There is, of course, an element of folklore regarding the moral status of life. Most physicians would say that the commitment to the preservation of life is essential to the Hippocratic tradition. Yet this principle is but a variant on Hippocratic medicine without classical roots. 'Only one important twentieth-century code', says Veatch, 'commits the physician to the preservation of life, the World Medical Association International Code of Medical Ethics, and that seems highly qualified with exceptions and seems targetted at the abortion issue rather than at contemporary problems in the care of the terminally ill.' (Veatch, 1984, pp. 22–3.) Preserving life may be a modern variant, grafted on to the physician's traditional duty to combat disease, but the link between certain diseases and death is obvious and the imperative to save life has been recognised since the earliest records of medical practice.

The reason why the moral status of life is central to the slippery slope argument is that the risk of opening the doors to those with less than a moral desire to kill is very real. The following analogy can make this point. Sometimes it may be necessary to punish a child for its own good and ultimate protection. One may hand out the punishment regretfully. But imagine someone rubbing his hands with glee at the prospect of legitimately inflicting punishment on a child. This is part of the case against corporal punishment; the sexual pleasure exhibited by some authorities makes it difficult to draw a boundary between those who would punish with the child's interest at heart and those who would punish out of their own interests. For this reason alternatives to corporal punishment are deemed necessary. No doubt certain offences may still require more severe punishment. But even if it were necessary to instil severe punishments, there is always something morally unpleasant in the pleasure which some Tory politicians have been known to produce among their supporters over the prospect of inflicting severe forms of punishment. The same can be said of mercy killing: it may be deemed necessary to kill, on occasions, out of a sense of mercy but that very motive might be corrupted by those with an interest in a more extended programme of killing.

That life has a moral value is hard to deny. The slippery slope begins when arguments are developed to prove that certain lives do not have any moral status. Often these arguments begin in the form of inquiries into what it is that makes life morally valuable. Now, the correct response is to assert that there are as many answers to the question as there are valuable lives. There is something fundamentally mistaken in the search for *the* most valuable feature of life, for here diversity will be the rule.

Instead of asking what is it that gives life a moral value, it is more constructive to consider what the overall effect would be if it were generally accepted that life had no value at all. This would entail acceptance of a world without moral value, without pity, compassion, hope and understanding, all of which depend upon the presumption that life has a moral status. Harris (1985) recognises the problems entailed in the attempt to discover reasons for giving life a value, and clearly opposes many proposals for the involuntary termination of life, but he does not capture the full significance of the imperative to value life, as we can see in the following passage:

> If we allow that the value of life for each individual consists simply in the those reasons, *whatever they are*, that each person has for finding their own life valuable and for wanting to go on living, then we do not need to know what the reasons are. All we need to know is that particular individuals have their own reasons, or rather, simply, that they value their own lives. (Harris, 1985, p. 16.)

As an argument against proposals for the involuntary termination of life Harris's remarks are obviously correct, but he fails to capture the absolute nature of the value of life which is sought by theorists who advocate a value of life principle. For Harris, it would appear, life only has the value which the individual concerned bestows upon it. His argument for the value of life will therefore turn on criteria for determining the capacity to value life, a position which is very far removed from the imperative to value all forms of life.

For Harris the capacity to value life is linked to the qualifying conditions for personhood. 'A person', says Harris, 'will be any being capable of valuing its own existence'. (Harris, 1985, p. 17.) Thus whatever value individuals bestow on their lives must be respected. A life that is valued should not be terminated, and a life that is not valued should not be prolonged. To frustrate the wishes of those who want to die will, on this view, insists Harris, 'be as bad as frustrating the will to live, for in each case we would be negating that value that individuals themselves put on their lives.' (Ibid., p. 17.)

46

The slippery slope objection to Harris's concept of a valued life is twofold: first, how do we know — for sure — that the life is not valued? Second, how do we know — in borderline cases involving dementia, adolescence, Down's Syndrome, overreaction to disease and pain, frustration in love affairs, and various forms of insanity — that the capacity to value life has not been impaired by these states? The force of the slope objection here is to focus attention on the criteria by means of which the capacity to value life can be determined. It may be that agreement will not be reached over criteria for an objective assessment that a person has a capacity to value life, or it may turn out that the discussion will become more and more involved with the borderline conditions concerning the capacity to value one's own life. If this happens then the slope argument will have achieved an important objective: it will have broadened the scope of moral concern from the proposal to the ethical and factual problems entailed in its implementation.

On Harris's terms there is a symmetry between being 'condemned to die' and being 'condemned to live' in that in both cases the individual's wishes may be flouted. On these terms it can be seen that, in the event of a conflict, the value of autonomy has greater priority than the value of life. Says Harris: 'To deny people the power of choice over their own destiny is to treat them as incompetent to run their lives . . .' (Harris, 1985, p. 80.) But in choosing autonomy over life Harris may be underrating the extent to which some people are — for various reasons — incompetent. Many of us have a great need for others to make important decisions for us, particularly so when the situation is unfamiliar or when we lack experience, or have a high regard for another person's competence in such matters. It is quite common when making career choices, facing emotional problems, making purchases, and choosing therapy options, to put greater trust in the wisdom of a loved one or friend than in one's own judgement. Paternalism is widely recognised in law; for example, laws concerning crash helmets for motorcyclists and seat-belts for motorists, and in the USA statutes which forbid the handling of dangerous snakes in religious rituals, and in the Indian government's attempt to prevent women from throwing themselves on their husband's funeral pyre. There is nothing irrational about this paternalism and it need not entail any significant loss of autonomy. Autonomy is an important factor when taking into consideration the moral status of other people, but there are many other moral requirements which can legitimately overrule it.

One of the fundamental problems with the atomistic concept of individual autonomy is that it neglects the extent to which the value individuals bestow on many things, including their lives, is mediated by the values bestowed on them by others. An individual may have no value for his or her life because the surrounding culture does not place any value on that individual's life. The high suicide rate among certain ethnic minorities and socially deprived groups serves as an illustration of the way in which the prevailing attitudes of a society can affect an individual's self-evaluation. In such cases it is extremely difficult to determine the extent to which a desire for death is autonomous. A jilted lover, or recently bereaved spouse, may view their situation as being 'condemned to live', but no therapist would recognise that an autonomous request for death was being expressed, for the very good reason that the majority of these cases recover. When faced with numerous borderline cases where it is hard to discern an autonomous motive (even if autonomy were a sufficient reason for death) it is hard to maintain any symmetry between being condemned to death and being condemned to live, since we can never be sure that all extraneous reasons have been eliminated from the choice in favour of death.

There is a further problem with the proposed symmetry between the two situations: a person can only be condemned to live for a finite time. Only Gods and magicians have the power to condemn someone to immortality; any fool can condemn someone to death, and that is a state which is infinite. It is, after all, the infinity of death which gives significance to the value of life principle and the fears of a wrongful death add credence to slippery slope warnings against any departure from this principle.

Suicide and the value of life

If it can be shown that an individual has a rational and genuine preference for death over life, and that the outcome of his life or death would not inflict great misery on others, then it would seem that the only argument against suicide is an absolutist form of the value of life principle which stresses that the taking of *any* life, for whatever reasons, is wrong. This is not a position which many would hold, but it is logical and defensible. Moreover, there is nothing fallacious about holding a principle that is rarely maintained in practice. It simply means that one subscribes to a moral ideal that few actually achieve, which is no reason for its rejection.

For many upholders of the value of life principle the act of suicide is wrong *a priori*. On the other hand, it is argued, that the prevention of suicide is a paternalistic infringement of an individual's rights. Moreover, it is alleged, that if a right to suicide is established then it follows that one has a right to assisted suicide (there is little point in granting rights if no assistance to fulfil them is permitted). Thus for the purpose of the following discussion no importance will be attached to the distinction between assisted and non-assisted suicide. The right to suicide — if such a right were recognised — must also entail the right to any assistance in fulfilling that right. Conversely objections to suicide must equally apply to both categories.

Perhaps the most commonly used slippery slope objection to suicide is that the granting of a right to suicide will lead to other more unacceptable consequences. It might be argued that if voluntary assisted suicide became morally permissible it would lead to a situation where enforced suicide of the elderly became commonplace. This is a 'horrible results' prediction which is obviously an exaggeration but nevertheless has two interpretations.

The first interpretation amounts to this: although suicide may be morally acceptable, enforced suicide of the elderly is not. The argument then is simply a matter of showing whether or not the former situation will lead to the latter.

The second interpretation is more complex. It suggests that the proposer of the argument is not only against the horrible result of enforced suicide, but also objects to voluntary suicide as well. Moreover, the objection to voluntary suicide need not entail any belief that it will necessarily lead to the enforced killing of the elderly. It may be sufficient to say that in an atmosphere where one form of taking life is commendable then its extension will flourish. It may be that the slippery slope argument is open to the charge that it cannot prove that A will necessarily lead to B, but it must be stressed that its opponents are also in the same position; they have no guarantee that it will not. But given the hostility and resentment towards certain groups in society it is by no means certain that more liberal attitudes towards suicide will not be abused. Perhaps the end stage of an assisted suicide programme will not result in the enforced killing of the elderly: 'one horrible result' however, might be the emergence of a society where no one cared about suicides.

One important feature of the slippery slope objections to suicide, either assisted or non-assisted, is that it warns of the dangers inherent in the libertarian standpoint whereby some individuals may find themselves irrationally caught up in the process. For there are problems in formulating criteria for determining when suicide is serious and when assistance is really wanted. There are problems in formulating criteria which will ensure that all subtle means of coercion have been eliminated. To avoid such problems it might be better to err on the side of a paternalist presumption in favour of life. Such a presumption might range from the refusal of assistance to a would-be-suicide to active intervention to prevent a successful suicide outcome.

However it is viewed, the right to commit suicide is the right to an irreversible state. For this reason it is important that such a right be exercised carefully. Since most people prefer life to death and take steps to avoid or postpone the latter, it can be presumed that the suicidal urge is a deviancy requiring explanation. At present, however, there is too little research into the urges which lead people to commit suicide. Whilst it must be conceded that many suicides fall outside the range of psychiatric concern, from the existing knowledge of psychiatric disorders underlying suicidal urges it is clear that many would-be suicides have been helped to complete recovery from the state which led them to seek death. It is, therefore, plausible to assume that with further research many more treatable psychiatric disorders may be found. This is not to say that all suicidal urges must be the outcome of psychiatric disorders (in some cases they may even be in response to psychiatric intervention): it is merely to recognise that, at the present state of knowledge, one cannot confidently rule them out. And since suicide is an irreversible cancellation of alternatives there is a justification behind the paternalistic attempt to combat it whenever possible. Instead of seeing the desperate state of the would-be suicide as an invitation to assist in a killing it might be more commendable to accept the responsibility to save a life and risk the charge of excessive paternalism.

In cases where death, possibly painful death, is inevitable then the issue of suicide is not central: the problem is simply when and how death shall occur. Consideration of suicide, like euthanasia, moves the discussion into the more controversial discussion *whether* death shall occur or not.

Against the foregoing paternalistic objections to suicide is the currently fashionable libertarian defence of suicide as an indi- vidual's ultimate expression of freedom. Many exponents of the 'right to suicide' speak of a free choice in this context, but they rarely specify alternatives. For them the choice is simply between dying or living, when the only alternative to suicide ever considered is more of a worthless painful life. But other alternatives might include praying, cursing, changing one's physicians or nurses, and many other possibilities.

High suicide rates among lower status groups, ethnic minorities, women and the non-voluntary unemployed indicate fundamental shortcomings in the suicide-as-an-individual's-right argument, since some individuals find themselves in an involuntary situation where suicide is more of an option than it would have otherwise been.

The key to the libertarian defence of suicide is the analogy between life and property. For Szasz (1977) there is an analogy between the property that a person has the right to dispose of and that person's life. Such a view might be seen as an advance beyond the theological ramifications of the sanctity of life argument, according to which an agent had no right to dispose of a life or a body that belongs to God, but it does so only if it lets in some form of dualism through the back door. But to say that suicide is wrong although you do not own your body or your life is not to say that God or anyone else owns it. Nobody owns it; unless one accepts a very crude form of dualism which postulates a disembodied state wherein something can decide how to dispose of one's life or body. The point worth noting is that life is not a property; it is the capacity to have experiences, which can neither be bought nor sold. Perhaps certain experiences can be purchased, but life, which is the state in which experiences take place, is not a disposable commodity.

4

The Contagiousness of Killing

According to Leo Alexander (1949), once we accept the concept of a life 'that is not worth living', we have stepped on to a slippery slope: any breach of the principle that all human life has a worth must have disastrous consequences. Marvin Kohl disagrees. His reply to the slope argument is found in his defence of euthanasia. Says Kohl:

> They maintain that if euthanasia is legalized, or even held to be moral, then all sorts of disastrous consequences will follow. We reply that it is equally possible that it may not be abused. Logically speaking the point is telling. Unfortunately, however, it is not persuasive. Following Joseph Fletcher we then ask: 'What is more irresponsible than to hide behind a logical possibility that is without antecedent probability?' (Kohl, 1974, p. 15.)

The weakness of the slope argument, argues Kohl, is in its appeal to logically possible consequences which are treated as empirical predictions. With logical consequences anything is possible so long as it is not self-contradictory. 'Since logical impossibility is an extremely limited kind of constraint', he says, 'it neither marks off nor prohibits inconfirmable, false, or conceptual sentences'. (Kohl, 1974, p. 16.) Hence we can say with equal impunity 'that man may run the mile in two minutes, or that he may not; and that euthanasia may lead to abuse, or that it may not.' (Ibid.)

The problem with Kohl's objection is that it rests on a caricature of the slope argument. The slope argument always requires a social context for its predictions to have significance. This is what Kohl has ignored. One of the essential functions of the slope argument is the manner in which it focuses attention on the moral significance of the act within the context of the social climate. Its moral significance is not in terms of logically possible consequences but in terms of plausible probabilities. Thus, for example, widespread information on contraception would not be considered a plausible route to the eventual extinction of humanity, although it might be said to be a logically possible route. Slopes have to be introduced against a background of likelihood. In a specific social context one may have very plausible grounds for an inference from the possible to the actual. Thus in the case of the Dutch physicians, who refused to be drawn into the arena of Nazi medical practice, there were very sound reasons for the expectation of further steps down the slope once the meaning and implications of the exclusive commitment to rehabilitation they were asked to sign were made clear to them. (See Chapter 2.) Kohl's rebuttal of the slope argument consists of opposing a prediction, which may be based on highly plausible grounds, with an argument designed to refute the fantasies permitted within the bounds of logical possibility.

However, this is not Kohl's central argument, which he reserves for what he sees as a stronger version of the slope argument. For a defender of a value of life principle 'one ought never to kill an innocent human being because such action *must* lead to undesirable consequences'. (Kohl, 1974, p. 17.) For Kohl this position amounts to the prediction that killing is ultimately contagious. It is important to note, however, that this formulation of the slope argument omits any reference to a specific social context, for it is a fact that in some situations killing may be contagious whereas in others it may not. Nevertheless, in rejecting the slope prediction of the contagiousness of killing Kohl appeals to 'overwhelming evidence indicating that human beings compartmentalise their experience and ideas; and that it is only when the normal process of compartmentalization breaks down that one encounters difficulties'. (Kohl, 1974, p. 19.) But here, too, a context is lacking. If one accidentally or unwillingly killed an assailant, it may not follow that one will become a habitual killer. But we can have reasons to fear contagion in cases where someone is attempting to overcome moral imperatives against the taking of human life. Soldiers who have been brutalised to the point where they have lost respect for life may become habitual killers, having lost the ability to compartmentalise their experiences. In the film, *The Godfather*, the young Michael contemplates the killing of Captain McClusky as a serious and final act; after the first killing the others were just 'business'.

Kohl's critique of the slope argument and subsequent defence of euthanasia rests ultimately on the thesis that human beings can limit their generalisations; the slope argument, on the other hand, draws attention to circumstances wherein the ability to limit generalisations has been lost. This is why the appeal to the ability to limit generalisations misses the point of the slope argument. We can see this in Kohl's presentation of the way humans compartmentalise experience and ideas. According to Kohl, the limit to a generalisation may be the concept of the 'same kind' or the 'same class'. 'If we crush an insect and believe it is a permissible act we do not believe that it is permissible to kill all living things. We conclude that it is permissible to kill this insect or at most, all kinds of insects.' (Ibid., p. 19.) Similarly, 'if we are taught to kill Nazis and the criteria for a Nazi and the circumstances of permissible killing are clearly spelled out, we do not kill all German nationals . . . We do not mistakenly generalise and kill all Europeans. Nor do we proceed either in fact or in mind to kill all human beings.' (Ibid., pp. 19–20.) Hence, 'the merciful killing of patients who want to die does not necessarily lead to the killing of the unwanted or the extermination of the human species'. (Ibid., p. 20.)

There are two problems with Kohl's appeal to our ability to compartmentalise. First, there is the problem of 'spelling out' the criteria for what shall constitute membership of a category, for this is the very problem which the slope argument raises. Even with the category of 'Nazi' there are severe problems: do we include all members of the Nazi party or exclude those who may have been coerced to join? And how do we define 'coercion'? Do we say that only those who felt a danger to their physical well-being were coerced, or do we include those whose research and careers would be adversely effected by refusal to join? As it happens, when it was considered permissible to kill Nazis it proved very difficult to compartmentalise the category of acceptable killing. Both politicians and the public in the Allied countries extended the category to include 'all German Nationals' when it suited them, as was shown in the bombing of of Dresden.

Second, it is pertinent to question whether categories can ever be as watertight as Kohl suggests. Even in wartime when the category for rightful killing may include only the enemy, there are genuine fears that soldiers will become desensitised to killing, and efforts are often taken to combat this before returning the soldiers to civilian life. When conceptual distinctions are considered abstractly, the appeal to compartments has plausibility, but in a social context there is a considerable blurring of the edges of conceptual distinctions. This is precisely what lies behind slope objections to the extension of certain categories. Thus Kohl may propose a new boundary out of a morally commendable motive to relieve suffering. But the force of the slope argument lies in the way it draws attention to the way in which new boundaries can be exploited by those with evil intentions. There is little doubt that the Nazi euthanasia policy was a travesty of merciful killing: that from the start their leaders had thought in terms of a larger scale of killing. But there is also evidence that they had realised that their programme would have to be introduced gradually, through the extension of newly accepted conceptual boundaries. People can be brutalised in a gradual process. With the Nazi euthanasia programme it was necessary to touch on the moral motives of those who genuinely wanted to kill out of a sense of mercy. But from the standpoint of those who wanted to 'clean up the Volk' it was a step in the right direction. Leo Alexander records how 'the German people were considered by the Nazi leaders more ready to accept the extermination of the sick than those for political reasons. It was for that reason that the first exterminations of the latter group were carried out under the guise of sickness.' (Alexander, 1949, p. 41.) Thus the conceptual boundaries of psychiatric sickness were redrawn to the point where they included 'inveterate German haters', namely prisoners who had been active in the Czech underground.

It is sometimes argued that the problem of the contagiousness of killing can be solved not merely by restricting the category of those to be killed, but by imposing limitations on those authorised to do the killing. According to Singer:

> If acts of euthanasia could only be carried out by a member of the medical profession, with the concurrence of a second doctor, it is not likely that the propensity to kill would spread unchecked throughout the community. Doctors already have a good deal of power over life and death, through their ability to withold treatment. There has been no suggestion that doctors who begin by allowing grossly defective infants to die from pneumonia will move on to withold antibodies from

racial minorities or political extremists. (Singer, 1983, p. 215.)

There are several problems with this argument. There would be major problems in obtaining widespread agreement among doctors to participate in the programme of killing and even to achieve a consensus that it is ethically permissible to allow grossly deformed infants to die. There may be a lot of hypocrisy regarding the adherence to principles which forbid the killing of grossly deformed infants and actual practices where subtle ways of killing take place, but moral hypocrisy is dependent upon the recognition of a principle, and the correct way to deal with hypocrisy is to adhere to the principle rather than to reject it. Singer has chosen to develop a case for euthanasia from a position which many of his opponents would see as halfway down the slope.

Whilst Kohl's criticism of the slope argument turns on the problem of drawing and maintaining conceptual boundaries, Singer's defence of euthanasia is formulated in the context of his programme for unsanctifying human life. (Singer, 1979.) According to Singer, the sanctity of life doctrine is nothing more than 'an arbitrary and unjustifiable distinction between our own species and other species'. (1979, p. 59.) The removal of this doctrine, he argues, would facilitate a situation where taking the lives of members of our own species, such as severely deformed infants, would be morally acceptable. Singer's reply to slippery slope objections to his proposal to unsanctify human life is as follows:

> People are liable to say that while the doctrine may be based on an arbitrary and unjustifiable distinction between our own species and other species, this distinction still serves a useful purpose. Once we abandon the idea, this objection runs, we have embarked on a slippery slope that may lead to a loss of respect for the lives of ordinary people and eventually to an increase in crime or to the selective killing of racial minorities or political undesirables. So the idea of sanctity of human life is worth preserving because the distinction it makes, even if inaccurate at some points, is close enough to a defensible distinction to be worth preserving. (Singer, 1979, p. 59.)

Singer then goes on to develop his reply to slippery slope predictions of the contagiousness of killing with an appeal to the ability to limit forms of killing, which rests on historical and anthropological evidence.

Ancient Greeks . . . regularly killed or exposed infants, but appear to have been at least as scrupulous about taking the lives of their fellow citizens as medieval Christians and modern Americans. In Eskimo societies it was the custom for a man to kill his elderly parents, but to murder a normal, healthy adult was virtually unknown. White colonialists in Australia would shoot aborigines for sport, as their descendants now shoot kangaroos with no discernible effect on the seriousness with which the killing of a white man was regarded. If we can separate such basically similar beings as aborigines and Europeans into distinct moral categories without transferring our attitude from one group to the other, there is surely not going to be much difficulty in marking off severely and irreparably retarded infants from normal human beings. Moreover, anyone who thinks that there is a risk of bad consequences if we abandon the doctrine of the sanctity of human life must still balance this possibility against the tangible harm to which the doctrine now gives rise: harm both to infants whose misery is needlessly prolonged and to non-humans whose interests are ignored. (Singer, 1979, pp. 59–60.)

On these terms the rebuttal of the slope argument is bound up with an appeal to the ability to compartmentalise experiences which rests, in turns, on a rather dubious form of ethical relativism. For if ancient Greeks practised infanticide, white Australians shot aborigines, and eskimos murdered their parents without any qualms, it would appear that they were so far down the slope that there would be little virtue to be derived from any appeal to the categories they excluded from acceptable killing. But what the appeal to ethical relativism in these examples of compartmentalism overlooks, is the fact that societies or even groups within societies, are not the homogeneous entities they are sometimes made out to be. Not every Greek supported infanticide, nor was genocide universally accepted by all white Australians, and parenticide could hardly be described as an eskimo custom; rather it was a desperate means of enhancing the survival of the group at the expense of its weaker members in conditions of extreme hardship. Consequently an improvement in material conditions should account for an end to the practice. Similar points can be made against Singer's remarks about the shooting of kangaroos: there has never been universal endorsement for species slaughter, and in the modern world opposition continues to increase. (In fact one of Singer's most important contributions to twentieth-century ethics has been his sustained attack on speciesism — the view that non-human animals exist only for the satisfaction of human desires.) These obvious facts concerning the lack of social homogeneity are frequently overlooked by both opponents and supporters of the slope argument, whose respective theses often rest on a crude homogeneous model of social change. Stage I pictures a society with no support for genocide. Stage II pictures one which permits certain forms of merciful killings. Stage III, however, is committed to a full policy of genocide. Some supporters of the slope argument have argued that the acceptance of Stage I will lead inevitably to Stages II and III, whereas their opponents claim that the line can be held at any stage. Against both views it is necessary to point out that societies are not unified in this way, and that within any given society at any given time there will be supporters and opponents of all three stages, plus many more besides. The plausibility of the slope argument is not based so much on the claim that Stage I must lead inevitably to Stage III, but rather from the claim that whilst the granting of Stage II may serve as a satisfactory position for those seeking no more than Stage II, it will nevertheless be seen as a partial victory for those committed to the realisation of Stage III.

It is important to stress this point against the tendency to think that the steps from legalising euthanasia to genocide are only taken in a Nazi culture, but not in the Western democracies. Kohl, for example, sees the Nazi culture as a counter-example to warnings against the possible contagious effects of killing people. The Nazis, he says, were acting in accord with a political ideology which rested on the principle that if the proper authorities believed that killing was good for Germany, then it was justifiable. As such he does not see the Nazi case as an example which will support the slope argument: 'Rather it is evidence that when men have almost unlimited power, their actions will be consistent with their beliefs, and when their beliefs entail needless cruelty, so will their actions.' (Kohl, 1974, p. 98.) This point is quite acceptable, but Kohl's overall argument rests on rather optimistic assumptions that the Nazi culture was wholly distinct from our own. In this respect the exponent of the slope argument is more realistic, recognising that there are within the Western democracies very real pressures eager to push in the direction of the Nazi programme. There may be an excess of the principle of pessimism — if the worst can happen it will — in the slope argument, but it serves as a counter to a dangerous naivety with regard to an easy dismissal of the suggestion that it 'might happen here'. To be sure genocide was the Nazis' objective from the beginning. No one should think that it began innocently out of proposals to alleviate suffering; although there were many humanitarians who were duped into supporting the initial stages of the programme for these reasons. Examples of this kind indicate a measure of support for any point on the slope, despite the fact that we do not live in a culture that is outwardly committed to a Nazi ideology. Appeals to the absolute value of life should not be lightly dismissed lest we lend encouragement to those with a total disregard for human life.

5

Voluntary Euthanasia

It is extremely difficult to argue against the case for voluntary euthanasia on behalf of a 'pain-racked', 'hopelessly incurable' cancer victim who has expressed a 'rational desire' to die. It has been argued, with considerable force, that the legalisation of voluntary euthanasia for patients in the above state will not lead down a slippery slope towards less acceptable forms of accelerated death. But one important aspect of the slope objection to voluntary euthanasia is a call to examine precisely what is meant by the expressions 'voluntary', 'pain-racked', 'hopelessly incurable' and 'rational desire'. At first sight the meaning of these terms appears intuitively obvious, but on closer examination they may yield fundamental ambiguities which may have serious consequences if incorporated into a proposal for euthanasia. Abstract propositions and carefully formed hypothetical situations are one thing in a philosophy seminar, law court, or legislative assembly, but deriving from them proposals to cover everyday situations in hospital wards are something else. The force and validity of the slope argument against voluntary euthanasia arises out of the inherent difficulties in translating principles into practice. On these terms one of the underlying strengths of the slope argument need not lie in the claim that there is something inherently wrong in every case of voluntary euthanasia, but rather it rests on the ability to pin-point the practical difficulties in the application of criteria for the implementation of the relevant principles.

According to the British voluntary euthanasia society, EXIT, voluntary euthanasia should be the 'lawful right of the individual, in carefully defined circumstances and with the utmost safeguards, if, and *only* if, that is his expressed wish'. (EXIT, 1980, p. 3.) This proposal is based on compassionate circumstances, and EXIT maintains that it does not entail 'getting rid of the old, the infirm and the unwanted . . .' nor 'the "putting down" of deformed children and mental defectives'. (EXIT, 1980, p. 3.)

There are two formulations of the slope objection, to these proposals; the empirical and the logical. The empirical objection takes the form of a prediction of further abuses which may or may not be substantiated in the fullness of time, whereas the latter objection raises fundamental logical objections which might never be surmounted. The empirical predictions can be seen in remarks by Sir Immanuel Jacobovits, who maintains that however freely it is decided, and however much it may be in the interests of the individual for the relief of suffering, voluntary euthanasia should be resisted in so far as it may be connected with a general cheapening of our respect for human life. Says Jacobovits:

> Once we compromise the infinite worth of every human life and make any human life finite in value, turning it from being absolute into becoming relative — either relative to his state of health or relative to his usefulness to society — this will automatically bring about a situation in which some human beings will be worth more and others worth less, ultimately leading to the Nazi doctrine whereby human beings were graded and shoved into gas ovens by the millions because they were inferior in value. (Jacobovits, 1974, p. 142.)

Whether this prediction is accurate or even relevant, and whether the analogy with Nazi Germany is relevant requires a consideration of issues already covered in Chapter II. Of immediate concern here are the logical problems which can be discerned in Jacobovits's blurring of the distinction between the different kinds of killing. How can we be certain that arguments for one kind of killing will not be used to support another kind of killing? How can we be sure that one kind of killing will not be confused with another? In the case of the criteria outlined by EXIT how can we be sure that the 'carefully defined circumstances' have been satisfactorily translated into practice? These logical objections raised by the slope argument are derived from what are often insoluble problems concerning the precise determination of the criteria for those 'carefully defined circumstances' according to which an individual may be deemed to have expressed a rational wish to die. It may also be discourteous to suggest that among EXIT's supporters there were those who favoured a looser interpretation of voluntary euthanasia than that advocated by other members. Were the provisions designed to prevent abuse sufficient to prohibit those whose attraction to euthanasia societies is questionable? How can we be sure that some of the more active euthanasia societies have not been infiltrated by those with an immoral interest in killing? To meet all of these objections one would have to devise further criteria for responsible membership of euthanasia societies. And so on. There is virtually no end to the demand for safeguards. To some, of course, these questions may be absurd, but they have to be asked if adequate safeguards are to be built into the 'carefully defined circumstances' according to which euthanasia can be permitted. Moreover, it may be imprudent to see any sinister motive behind EXIT's decision to include, in an appendix to one of their leaflets advocating euthanasia, a form of 'wording of bequest', with instructions for bequeathing a sum of money to the society in the event of one's death. It may seem paranoid to suggest that societies promoting voluntary euthanasia have unpleasant ulterior motives, or have been infiltrated by unscrupulous characters. But equally so — and this is an important aspect of the slope argument — there are no compelling reasons as to why we should not fear such motives. Throughout history organisations devoted to charity and peace have been infiltrated by those who have advocated hate and war. The record of such organisations being subverted by those with less merciful objectives is a dismal testimony of slippery slides. The subversion of Christian values in the excesses of the Inquisition; frequent reports of the infiltration of peace movements by *agent provocateurs*, and even the infiltration of high offices in the United Nations by prominent ex-Nazis, indicate the extent to which organisations established with one set of values might unwittingly nurture those with very different values. The question posed by the slope argument is how can we prevent the reasons for merciful killing from being hijacked by the merciless?

Yale Kamisar, an exponent of the slope objection to voluntary euthanasia, outlines the strongest and most unshakable set of criteria for the authorisation of euthanasia. Yet, as we shall see, they do not overcome the slope objection. The criteria Kamisar considers is as follows:

If a person is *in fact* i) presently incurable, ii) beyond the aid of any respite which may come along in his life expectancy, suffering iii) intolerable and iv) unmitigable pain and of a v) fixed and vi) rational desire to die. (Kamisar, 1983, p. 458.)

It is certainly hard to imagine a form of words that would express a serious moral objection to the above criteria for voluntary euthanasia. Yet, as Kamisar observes, abstract propositions, however carefully formed, are one thing; their application is something else. Once the abstract conditions are established, a physician is then left to use his or her good sense and judge on the basis of past experience. This is Kamisar's objection; whilst most physicians have good sense, some do not. Some are inexperienced, some are plain stupid. What counts as 'good sense' is hard to define and is often harder to identify. Good sense may be morally commendable, but how does one acquire it? It is generally agreed that it is acquired through experience. If so, then how much experience? Young and inexperienced physicians may acquire good sense through the recognition of their mistakes. Are mistakes in the application of criteria for euthanasia to be regarded as an acceptable means of acquiring good sense? Given the fact that errors in decisions relating to voluntary euthanasia may involve needless loss of life, an appeal to good sense is far too risky to merit a fundamental change in our homicide laws.

In this respect the appeal to slippery slopes draws attention to the following problems: on the one hand there is a need for euthanasia in genuine cases, but how can the implementation of the proposal provide guarantees against: (1) the incidence of mistake and abuse; and (2) the danger that legal machinery initially designed for killing those who are a nuisance to themselves may some day engulf those who are a nuisance to others.

Voluntary euthanasia and the right to life

For some philosophers the case in favour of voluntary euthanasia is so powerful that it is puzzling why there should be any moral objections to it at all. Michael Tooley finds it rather puzzling as to why the slope argument should be employed as an objection to voluntary euthanasia for a person who has a 'rational desire that his life be terminated'. (Tooley, 1979, p. 68.) For Tooley the philosophical problem is not so much a question of justifying euthanasia as one of examining the reasons why 'many people view voluntary euthanasia as morally objectionable'. (Ibid.) According to Tooley the main reason why the slope argument is employed against voluntary euthanasia is because it is seen as a threat to the sanctity of life. There are, as we have seen in Chapter III, several religious aspects of the sanctity of life principle, but Tooley does not see these as constitutive of any stumbling block. The belief that we have an obligation to go on living out of duty to a Creator can be summarily dismissed by denying the existence of a Creator. But the version of the slope argument against euthanasia which attracts Tooley's attention can be found in the frequently quoted remarks by G. K. Chesterton:

> Some people are proposing what is called euthanasia; at present only a proposal for killing those who are a nuisance to themselves; but soon to be applied to those who are a nuisance to other people. (Chesterton, 1937, p. 486.)

Tooley's reply consists of a rebuttal of the prediction that killing those who want to be killed will lead to the killing of those who do not want to be killed. He says:

> If someone were to advocate sexual activity, and a critic were to object that while only voluntary sexual activity is being advocated at present, the proposal will soon be extended to cover compulsory sexual activity, i.e., rape, the critic would hardly be taken seriously. If the analogy is a fair one, the objection is surely preposterous. (Tooley, 1979, p. 69.)

But is this a fair analogy? In the case of euthanasia the slope objection rests on the belief that one form of killing is not significantly distinct from another, and that it may not be that easy to maintain a distinction in practice between the two forms of killing. In Tooley's analogy, however, the distinction between sexual activity and rape is less problematic. For the analogy only holds if rape is regarded as a form of sexual activity, albeit an involuntary one. But if it is accepted that rape is not primarily a form of sexual activity but a violent assault, with injuries directed at sexual organs, then the analogy breaks down.

However, Tooley is on stronger ground when he accuses exponents of the slippery slope argument of failing to distinguish between (1) arguments for the sanctity of life and (2) arguments for the right to life. It does not follow, argues Tooley, that a rejection of the principles underlying the sanctity of life will necessarily entail a rejection of the principles underlying the right to life. According to the right of life principle, every human being has a right to life, but this does not mean that it is always wrong to kill a human being. Moreover, argues Tooley, one can reject the sanctity of life principle without having any commitment to the view that no one has a right to life, or that decisions to terminate a life should be based on concepts of social utility. One can argue for the right to life whilst insisting on other rights, such as the right to terminate one's own life, or the right to assisted suicide. Thus, for Tooley, the slope can be avoided once it is recognised that one can maintain a commitment to voluntary euthanasia whilst at the same time, supporting the right to life and opposing compulsory euthanasia.

The distinction is very important and it certainly disposes of a slope argument based exclusively on an appeal to the sanctity of life principle. But it does not dispose of a stronger version of the slope argument which can be applied even when one recognises a distinction between voluntary euthanasia and euthanasia based on concepts of social utility. For there is the problem of distinguishing between arguments for euthanasia on grounds of social utility — which on Tooley's terms is morally unacceptable — and arguments for euthanasia on grounds of social utility which are employed by someone who endorses the right to life in Tooley's sense — which is morally acceptable. It is not hard to imagine someone opting for euthanasia because he has come to perceive his life as being a nuisance to others. (This is the ultimate substance of Chesterton's remarks, although it is not fully articulated.) It is perfectly possible for someone to see himself as a nuisance to himself precisely because he *has* become a nuisance to others. It is very hard to maintain a clear distinction between judging the uselessness of one's own life and someone else's judgement regarding the uselessness of the life in question. In a very important sense our opinions of ourselves are often grounded on the opinions of others. Nowhere is this phenomenon stronger than when forming attitudes about ourselves: the value placed on one's own life is a product of the value others attribute to it. In this respect it is extremely difficult, in practice, to separate concepts of social utility from a free and autonomous decision regarding the worth of one's own life.

Tooley stresses that it is possible to maintain a distinction between the right to life and the right to voluntary euthanasia on the one hand, from social utility arguments for euthanasia on the other hand. But such a distinction abstractedly defined is rendered useless in practice when one is confronted with a person who says: 'Although I respect the right to life and insist equally on the right for voluntary euthanasia and assisted suicide, my criterion for euthanasia in my own case is when I am deemed to be a nuisance to to others.' This is not uncommon. Many of our elderly citizens find the prospect of being a nuisance to others intolerable. In such cases the notion of social utility is part of the individual's criteria for the exercise of the right to assisted suicide. It is clearly a step further down the slope towards less acceptable motives for killing than Tooley's formulation intends. Yet such a position is entirely compatible with Tooley's formulation of the criteria for voluntary euthanasia.

By pushing the argument to the point where a request for voluntary euthanasia is hardly distinguishable from the killing of those who have been encouraged to see that they are a nuisance to others and that they should opt for euthanasia, the exponent of the slope argument is drawing attention to a very serious moral question which is too often ignored. To what extent does voluntary euthanasia rule out alternatives? In the case of a person who perceives himself as a nuisance to himself because he is a nuisance to others, voluntary euthanasia may block off the morally significant fact that there is something valuable in the life of a nuisance.

One of the problems with appeals to rights, such as the 'right to life' is that there is often a presumption that rights have to be either earned or that they depend upon the possession of some faculty or aptitude. Thus to maintain the right to life, like the right to treatment, one must subscribe to certain beliefs and behaviour patterns. Accordingly the right to life may be contingent, whereas the value of life principle admits of no qualification. Shorn of the theological infrastructure of the sanctity of life principle an absolute value of life is preferable to the right to life. (See Chapter 3.)

The extent to which a person's nuisance rating can be incorporated into judgements concerning the continuance of life-sustaining therapy can be seen in the case of a patient in an Oxford hospital in 1985 who was taken off kidney dialysis. The head of the renal unit was reported to have said in defence of the decision that the patient, Mr Sage

   . . . is mentally defective and schizophrenic. He did not fit the criteria for dialysis. He has progressively deteriorated from that point in that he became virtually mute and unable to look after himself. He became abusive and he was not looked after properly. We had to feed him. He had to be cleaned up from urine and faeces and then sedated. He hit other patients. He hit staff. (*Guardian*, 8 January 1985.)

In this case the patient's nuisance rating appears to have been an important factor in an ethically dubious decision that 'the patient's quality of life was not good enough to justify dialysis'. (A spokesman for Oxford Authority, quoted in the *Guardian*, 8 January 1985.)

Notwithstanding the complexities of the case it would seem that the withdrawal of life-supporting facilities, in a situation where death is an inevitable outcome of such action, would constitute a case of passive involuntary euthanasia. This is why the decision to withdraw Mr Sage from kidney dialysis was greeted with such an outcry. The case also reveals the inherent indeterminacy of decisions based on hypotheses about the quality of a patient's life. Whereas the health authorities suggested that the patient's quality of life did not justify dialysis, the patient's own doctor was quoted as saying that he was a 'happy and much loved member of the community'. (*Guardian*, 9 January 1985.) Members of Parliament called for an inquiry (ibid.) and the National Council for Civil Liberties took up the case on behalf of Mr Sage. (*Guardian*, 11 January 1985.) Eventually, the British Kidney Patient's Association intervened and arranged for therapy to be provided at St John and St Elizabeth's Hospital, North London, until 25 April 1985, when Mr Sage died of a stroke after hearing of his mother's death. (*The Times*, 26 April 1985.)

Among the factors underpinning the opposition to the decision to withdraw Mr Sage from kidney dialysis was the fact that the decision appeared to be based on the claim that the patient was a nuisance to others. But our moral obligation to save the lives of nuisances is not lessened by the fact that they have come to see themselves as nuisances to themselves. Instead, the moral challenge here is to make them less of a nuisance both to themselves and to others.

Voluntary euthanasia as an expression of human freedom

It is often argued that voluntary euthanasia is a question of prime importance to those concerned with civil liberties. Glanville Williams (1967) sees voluntary euthanasia as an important aspect of human liberty.

> If the law were to remove its ban on euthanasia, the effect would be merely to leave the subject to the individual conscience. The proposal would . . . be easy to defend, as restoring personal liberty in a field in which men differ on the question of conscience . . . On a question like this there is surely everything to be said to the liberty of the individual. (Williams, cited by Kamisar, 1983, p. 459.)

But whilst it is hard to formulate any serious moral objections against an extension of civil liberties there is a crucial problem in identifying a 'free' decision. Excluded from this category — and hence from decisions regarding voluntary euthanasia — would be many casualties of strain, pain, or narcotics. (Kamisar, 1983, p. 459.) In the absence of any clear-cut objective criteria for drawing a distinction between those who genuinely desire death and those whose desire is only apparent, there will be an inevitable risk of starting on a slope which begins with a proposal to extend individual freedom and ends in the ultimate extinction of freedom.

According to Kamisar, proposals for voluntary euthanasia raise the problem of drawing up a balance sheet between the denial of civil liberties to those who may require euthanasia on the grounds that it avoids mistakenly including those who may not genuinely wish to die, and granting euthanasia along with the risk of infringing the liberties of those who irrationally get caught up in the process. Confronted with such a balance Kamisar concludes, on utilitarian grounds, against the legalisation of voluntary euthanasia.

> My price on behalf of those who, despite appearances to the contrary, have some relatively normal and reasonably useful life left to them, or who are incapable of making the choice, is the lingering on for a while of those who, if you will, *in fact* have no desire and no reason to linger on . . . (Kamisar, 1983, p. 459.)

It is all too easy to include, in a voluntary euthanasia programme, those whose decisions do not express a genuine desire for accelerated death. To what extent should a patient in severe pain and stress be deemed capable of expressing a rational desire for death? A patient in severe pain may be administered narcotics. Later the patient may develop a tolerance to them. In such cases when is the patient to make the choice? Should it be whilst experiencing severe pain, whilst heavily drugged, or is narcotic relief to be withdrawn for the time of the decision? 'But', asks Kamisar, 'if heavy dosage no longer deadens pain, indeed no longer makes it bearable, how overwhelming is it when whatever relief narcotics offer is taken away too?' (Kamisar, 1983, p. 459.) Mental impairment is a noted feature of narcotic dosage. A cancer patient on morphine may be dependent upon it and react to withdrawal with an addict's responses.

Apart from narcotics it is well-known that pain distorts judgement. And there are some individuals who would scream for death after an experience of only minor discomfort. Others experiencing severe pain may make an irrational judgement in a moment of despair. It is often said that there are lucid moments in certain disease processes. This need not be denied. The problem lies in devising criteria by means of which they can be clearly detected.

But even if the problem of ascertaining the influence of narcotics or severe pain could be resolved there still remains the fact that the scope of voluntary decisions is necessarily undetermined. A voluntary decision depends on the amount of information at one's disposal regarding alternatives. This, in turn, depends on the amount of information which the physician possesses and the ability of the physician to communicate this information. Here the difference between the experienced and the inexperienced physician may be crucial. There is also the problem that in less affluent communities, where the quality of medical services and advice is below average, decisions regarding euthanasia will be less informed and ergo less voluntary than those reached in the better off communities.

In daily life most voluntary acts have a built in reversibility. A voluntary credit plan can be terminated within a certain period. This protects the customer from hasty decisions and undue pressure. In some cases it is the very mechanism for reversing the decision which guarantees its voluntary status. Voluntary hospitalisation can be rescinded at the patient's request. One can rescind an irrational decision in favour of a rational course or rescind a rational decision in favour of an irrational course. The rationality of the decision is not the issue: what matters most, from the moral standpoint, is that in many cases, where harm is a probable outcome, voluntary decisions should have built in safeguards for reversibility. But the problem with voluntary euthanasia is that once it is activated no reversal is possible.

The problem of what constitutes an 'incurable condition' likewise yields innumerable borderline cases. Obviously a patient in an advanced state of cancerous toxemia is incurable. But then such a patient is disqualified from proposals concerning voluntary euthanasia since he or she would be beyond the stage where rational decisions could be formulated. Moreover, the uncertainty regarding the diagnosis of certain 'incurable states' is partly why terms like 'chronic' and 'persistent' have replaced terms like 'incurable'. Transplants and associated techniques have also radically transformed whole categories of what were hitherto considered as 'incurable states'.

Even if the decision that the condition is incurable is beyond all doubt, there is still the problem of those who choose to exercise their civil rights because they (rightly or wrongly) perceive themselves as an unwarranted burden on others. An extension of civil rights in favour of a legal option for euthanasia can so easily include those who may not normally choose it.

On balance, it would seem, there are very strong utilitarian grounds for restricting the right to a voluntary accelerated death. Nevertheless, there is no shortage of utilitarian argument in favour of voluntary euthanasia. Singer rebuts several utilitarian objections with his own utilitarian defence of voluntary euthanasia. On balance, it would seem, there *is* a utilitarian case for euthanasia.

It is often said, in debates about euthanasia, that doctors can be mistaken. Certainly some patients diagnosed by competent doctors as suffering from an incurable condition have survived. Possibly the legalization of voluntary euthanasia would, over the years, mean the deaths of one or two people who would have otherwise recovered. This is not, however, the knockdown argument against euthanasia some people imagine it to be. Against a very small number of unnecessary deaths that might occur if euthanasia is legalized we must place the very large amount of pain and distress that will be suffered by patients who really are terminally ill if euthanasia is not legalized. (Singer, 1983, p. 212.)

Singer's utilitarian balance, no doubt, could be invoked to justify an occasional injection of deadly virus in an unwilling patient, provided that this action would be offset by the alleviation of a 'very large amount of pain and distress' that would otherwise be suffered. This is the inherent weakness of Kamisar's appeal to a utilitarian based argument against voluntary euthanasia. For if it turns out, on balance, that greater liberty, or greater happiness, actually does result from the practice of voluntary euthanasia, then one has to provide other kinds of objections if one is to maintain a consistent resistance to euthanasia. If one's central objection to voluntary euthanasia is based on the possibility of unnecessary deaths then arguments which stress the wrongness of euthanasia must be based on other principles than utilitarianism. For the most part, however, it should be sufficient to demonstrate that unecessary deaths are a likely consequence of euthanasia. If that is not seen as an overriding moral problem there is little further moral sanction to be derived from an appeal to the slippery slope or to borderline cases.

There is a very important strand of thought, according to which human freedom has greater priority than life. Fierce campaigns have been conducted on behalf of those who value the freedom to pursue dangerous activities, such as boxing, hang-gliding, pot-holing, and the consumption of alcohol and various drugs. On the scale of human happiness, so it would seem, life has a very low priority. Against those who would advocate that the individual should be left to pursue his or her interests free from external interference slope arguments are paternalistic. And in one important respect the slope objection to voluntary euthanasia has an element of paternalism which is similar to the arguments employed in favour of the prohibition of dangerous activities. Now, it must be conceded that the slope argument *is* paternalist and that a defence of the slope argument must also defend a limited form of paternalism. To put it as clearly as possible: despite all the libertarian objections, exponents of the slippery slope argument accept that there are times when we may not know what is in our interests, and that as a rule a presumption in favour of life should override the expressed wishes of an individual. It should also be stressed in this context that the outright rejection of paternalism is the abandonment of moral discourse in favour of radical subjectivism. Without some claims to know what is best for others there could be no basis for moral discourse. What slippery slope objections to voluntary euthanasia maintain is that certain consequences of an act may not always be apparent to the agent concerned. In many areas of life it may be prudent for the paternalistic well-wisher to leave the agent to make his or her mistakes, on the basis that autonomy and the value of learning from one's mistakes is essential to the individuals's sense of dignity and self-respect. But decisions regarding life and death have a finality about them which may, in some circumstances, weigh heavier than dignity and self-respect.

If it is established that individuals have a right to die by virtue of their autonomy, then this right need not be tied to situations where pain and suffering is alleged to be intolerable. If one adopts the principle that death is the individual's inalienable right then the issue whether one is in pain or not is merely contingent. According to Singer, even if it were possible to eliminate pain and for all patients to be guaranteed a painless death, it would still be wrong to prohibit a patient from expressing this right. Says Singer:

> Perhaps one day it will be possible to treat all terminally ill patients in such a way that no one requests euthanasia and the subject becomes a non-issue; but this still-distant prospect is no reason to deny euthanasia to those who die in less comfortable conditions. It is, in any case, highly paternalistic to tell dying patients that they are now so well looked after that they need not be offered the option of euthanasia. It would be more in keeping with respect for individual freedom and autonomy to legalize euthanasia and let patients decide whether their situation is bearable — let them, as Derek Humphrey puts it, have the dignity of selecting their own endings. (Singer, 1983, p. 212.)

These remarks have considerable merit. There is an element of unwarranted paternalism in attempts to frustrate a patient's known wishes. But there are fundamental problems which are not easily dealt with by uttering the slogan 'let them decide whether their situation is bearable'. First, there are genuine reasons, based on sound experience, that the disease process, reaction to drugs, ignorance of the total situation, and even hospitalisation, may affect the decision. Second, demands for an individual's right to choose can usually be met without recourse to euthanasia. In many of the cases cited by euthanasia societies in favour of accelerated death, the individual could exercise the right to refuse certain therapeutic measures. This right is not equivalent to euthanasia (see Chapter VI), and eliminates the problems entailed in framing a statutory right to assisted suicide. The third problem is related to Singer's charge of paternalism against those who prohibit euthanasia. There are, of course, many areas when an individual's wishes are respected, even if the results are fatal. Gluttony, heavy alcohol consumption and cigarette smoking, all are legally accepted ways of accelerating one's death. One of the reasons why they are not prohibited is that health agencies can, in principle, counsel and advise people to break off these life-endangering practices. (Other reasons, such as political pressure from the manufacturers of these products need not be discussed here.) Some dangerous practices, like heroin consumption, are considered irreversibly destructive and are prohibited. Heroin addiction is not a legal right. This may be, for some, a restriction on individual freedom, but the broad consensus of moral opinion favour the outlawing of heroin. If the prevention of heroin addiction is a justifiable form of paternalism then, presumably, the prevention of euthanasia could be deemed to be an equally justifiable form of paternalism.

Singer rejects the analogy between the paternalistic prohibition of heroin addiction and the prohibition of euthanasia. Heroin addiction, he argues, is prohibited because it falls into a category of free acts which are not rationally based. Voluntary euthanasia on the other hand, he argues, is seen to be acceptable if it is based on a rational decision. This argument, of course, turns on the problem of what is to count as a rational decision. In the light of Kamisar's arguments concerning the problem of determining whether decisions made by terminally ill patients are rational, it would seem that the slippery slope argument has particular weight against Singer's proposal. Moreover, Singer's point that heroin addiction is not based on a rational decision is an assertion without foundation. He does not provide evidence to show that heroin addicts are less rational than those who request voluntary euthanasia. In fact, one of the problems which those who campaign against heroin addiction will have to face — if their campaign is serious — is that heroin addicts are capable of producing very convincing arguments in defence of their habit — one of them being the inconsistency in the toleration of killers like alcohol and nicotine whilst prohibiting heroin. And the fact that heroin consumers are willing to provide reasons in defence of their addiction seems to have escaped the attention of those responsible for the promotion of the anti-heroin campaign. Among addict communities these reasons are compelling, even if morally deplorable. Yet, according to Singer, heroin addition falls into a category of acts which 'are obviously not rationally based and which we can be sure they will later regret. (Singer, 1983, p. 213.) This, he argues, is why paternalism is justified when combatting heroin addiction. But if the concept of 'irrationality' is linked to the making of decisions which will later be regretted, then voluntary euthanasia is rational only because the agent will no longer be around to regret it. However, it is precisely because it will be too late to regret it that objections to euthanasia are made. Most serious minded people have little sympathy for the argument that a period of heroin addiction enriches one's experience of life. One may tolerate, but not seriously accept, such an argument, hoping all the time that the would-be addict will come to his or her senses before too much damage is inflicted. But with euthanasia no such a compromise is possible. And this is why an absolutist stance is adopted by those who oppose it.

In a very important sense the question of rationality is beside the point when formulating objections to either heroin addiction or voluntary euthanasia. One can conceive of rational arguments for and against both practices. A life may be deemed so miserable that either addiction or death may seem preferable. The addict may appeal to a momentary pleasure in a life of utter misery, a chance to forget — all of those clichés have been exploited to the full by utilitarian defenders of heroin consumption. And the difference between these arguments and those in favour of voluntary euthanasia is insignificant.

The attempt to found the morality of voluntary euthanasia on rational decisions is misguided. Rational decisions can be overturned after further deliberation. There are no grounds for the assumption that a rational decision in favour of accelerated death has to be permanent. Its permanence can only be guaranteed by the execution of the decision. There is no reason to assume that when a rational decision has been made it must be the only one. We can have conflicting rational decisions.

It is sometimes argued that there is an element of moral hypocrisy attached to arguments against voluntary euthanasia whilst no significant objections are made on behalf of the thousands of patients who suffer and die unnecessarily from heart disease, kidney failure, and hypothermia, because of a parsimonious attitude on behalf of governments and welfare agencies. Harris (1985, pp. 85–6) cites, what he describes as, the 'British government's euthanasia programme' in this context. This 'massive administration of non-voluntary and involuntary euthanasia', says Harris, 'is the result of government policy or action'. (Harris, 1985, p. 85.)

Now Harris's reference to a 'euthanasia programme' might be dismissed as hyperbole were it not for the available authoritative medical sources which can be cited. Among those cited by Harris is an instruction from a health authority to 'turn away patients dying of kidney failure because the authority has run out of money', which one consultant, Dr Daniel Glyn Williams, described as 'effectively an order to allow patients to die within weeks or within months at the most'. (Cited by Harris, 1985, p. 85.) Harris goes on to cite authoritative sources which indicate that at least 2,000 patients suffering from kidney disease alone die each year because sufficient treatment is not available. As Harris says: 'All of these people and thousands more, have died as a direct and avoidable consequence of decisions taken by government about which they are not consulted and to which they do not consent.' (Ibid.)

Now Harris is obviously correct in drawing attention to the calumny of a government that has maintained an implicit euthanasia policy, in the form of a restriction of life-maintaining services, which has to be seen as an annual cull of the long-term diseased, the aged and poor. More recent evidence in support of Harris's argument comes from a consultant geriatrician at St Pancras Hospital, London, who estimated in 1986 that 'for every degree below average in Winter . . . there is an extra 8,000 deaths'. (*Observer*, 3 March 1986.) Deaths from hypothermia and diseases and injuries relating to inadequate heating and diet are indicative of the fashionable belief that provisions for the aged and less fortunate should have a low priority. But although these facts clearly condemn governments, welfare agencies, and complacent members of the public, as participants in forms of irresponsible killing of the innocent, the open endorsement of voluntary euthanasia can hardly be seen as an alternative to this kind of moral hypocrisy. The correct course for anyone committed to a value of life argument is to openly and strongly condemn the government's euthanasia programme. It might even be said, from the standpoint of the slope argument, that were euthanasia legalised, it would even lend a degree of respectability to the government's 'euthanasia programme'.

The merits of the slope argument against voluntary euthanasia lie, not so much in a prediction that it will actually and inevitably lead to involuntary euthanasia, but rather in its recognition that, on close inspection, the line between voluntary and involuntary decisions is extremely hard to maintain. In so far as the slope argument draws on the appeal to a 'value of life' principle this need not commit the exponent of the slope argument to any theological doctrine concerning the sanctity of life. It is sufficient that the slope exponent draws attention to the irreversible nature of decisions to authorise death. It is the finality of death, rather than the slippery slope, that tips the balance against voluntary euthanasia. As long as conceptual and practical uncertainty remains, the finality of death is the ultimate reason for the presumption in favour of life.

6

The Right to Refuse Treatment

One area where an accelerated death may not lead down the slippery slope to unacceptable modes of killing is in the fulfilment of the right to refuse treatment. But it is only when this right is unhampered by cost-benefit considerations that the slope can be avoided. The right to refuse treatment, even to the point of death, is not synonymous with assisted suicide. In the first place, a refusal of treatment may not be accompanied with a desire to die. A refusal to accept intervention on religious grounds, even when it proves fatal, need not be accompanied with a desire to die. The patient may be willing to undergo alternatives — however ludicrous they may appear to orthodox opinion — or the patient may have a strong wish to recover, even pray for Divine intervention, but not be willing to accept the therapy that has been proposed by the attending physician. The would-be suicide, on the other hand, will not consider *any* form of treatment, will not wish for Divine intervention, preferring death as the only possible outcome. From the standpoint of the physician the patient's refusal of therapy, even when death is inevitable, does not involve complicity in an act of passive euthanasia, since the refusal may be against his or her advice and intentions. To be prevented from saving the life of a patient who refuses treatment may be very tragic, but with possible exceptions of nagging doubts that one could have been more persuasive, the outcome falls into the same category as situations where a physician was not consulted in time, where a willingness to help was frustrated by external circumstances.

Refusal of treatment and passive euthanasia

On 4 December 1973, the House of Delegates of the American Medical Association (AMA) issued the following statement originally intended as a distinction between cases involving extraordinary and ordinary care, but it also drew an implicit distinction between cases where a physician authorises cessation of therapy and cases where it is legitimate for the patient to authorise cessation of therapy:

> The intentional termination of the life of one human being by another — mercy killing — is contrary to that for which the medical profession stands and is contrary to the policy of the American Medical Association.
>
> The cessation of the employment of extraordinary means to prolong the life of the body when there is irrefutable evidence that biological death is imminent is the decision of the patient and/or his immediate family. The advice and judgement of the physician should be freely available to the patient and/or his immediate family. (Cited by Steinbock, 1983, p. 290.)

Opposition to this statement focused on the allegation that it expresses a morally significant distinction between active and passive euthanasia, whereby the AMA were seen to be prohibiting active euthanasia while allowing, under certain conditions, passive euthanasia. (Rachels, 1983.) The same allegation was made by Tooley, who also took the AMA statement as a prohibition of active euthanasia, whilst endorsing certain forms of passive euthanasia:

> Many people hold that there is an important moral distinction between passive euthanasia and active euthanasia. Thus, while the AMA maintains that people have a right 'to die with dignity', so that it is morally permissible for a doctor to allow someone to die if that person wants to and is suffering from an incurable illness causing pain that cannot be sufficiently alleviated, the AMA is unwilling to countenance active euthanasia for a person who is in similar straits, but who has the misfortune not to be suffering from an illness that will result in a speedy death. (Tooley, 1983, p. 290.)

One of the problems in this case is caused by the confusing terminology employed by the AMA. They used ambiguous terms, like 'bodily life' and 'biological death', which indicates an element of fudge with regard to their concept of death. An endorsement of a clearly defined concept of brain death (Lamb, 1985) would eliminate this ambiguity and the AMA need not appear to be endorsing any form of euthanasia, simply recognising a moment when further attempts to maintain the viability of certain organs would be futile. Clearly defined criteria for death, and hence criteria for the cessation of efforts to maintain the semblance of life in the body, would avoid the AMA's apparent endorsement of euthanasia which, according to the spirit of their opening sentence, is clearly unacceptable to them.

But leaving aside the need for clarity regarding the concept of death, are both Rachels and Tooley correct in seeing support for passive euthanasia — or even in seeing a distinction between passive and active euthanasia — in the AMA statement?

According to Steinbock, Tooley and Rachels are mistaken in their identification of the cessation of life-prolonging treatment with passive euthanasia, or intentionally letting die. The tendency to see an endorsement of passive euthanasia in the AMA statement, however, is bound up with the mistaken identification of giving up life-prolonging therapy with passive euthanasia. As Steinbock points out:

> If it were right to equate the two, then the AMA statement would be self-contradictory, for it would begin by condemning, and end by allowing, the intentional termination of life. But if cessation of life prolonging treatment is not always or necessarily passive euthanasia, then there is no confusion and no contradiction. (Steinbock, 1983, p. 290.)

In a very important sense, ceasing therapy, giving up when the situation is hopeless, is not a form of euthanasia. (Lamb, 1985.) In such circumstances there may be little else that a physician can do. In many cases therapy may be terminated without any intention to cause death on the physician's part. The circumstances might be such that the treatment stands little or no chance of improving the condition and may possibly bring about greater suffering than relief. No physician has an ethical obligation to persist with useless therapy.

This is particularly important in cases when a patient invokes a right to refuse treatment; it need not be the same as a request for the right to assisted suicide. A patient dying of an incurable disease may wish to remove himself from a set of therapeutic procedures that may sustain life. That patient might wish for accelerated death or wish for a miraculous recovery; the motives are irrelevant. The patient may simply argue that he or she has no wish to prolong a set of procedures which are causing misery. According to Rachels and Tooley this would not be significantly different to the physician administering a lethal dose. Yet although the outcome may be the same, there is an important difference between on the one hand the administration of a fatal dose or the witholding of life-sustaining therapy, and a patient's refusal of life-prolonging treatment on the other hand. The distinction turns on a fundamental issue; the patient's right to refuse treatment, which is bound up with other rights held by the living such as freedom from assault, wrongful incarceration, and so on. Unlike assisted suicide the right to the refusal of treatment does not require a situation where one human being is involved in the killing — by act or omission — of another human being. It is a right which has been upheld in numerous cases, although borderline examples can be found in cases where the disease in question may have adverse effects on others. These borderline cases are confined to carefully defined circumstances where the rights of the individual are superseded with reference to wider interests. Thus, partly in response to the panic over the disease AIDS, on 20 February 1985 the British government took powers to forcibly detain in hospital certain individuals affected by dangerous diseases. The government stopped short of making AIDS a notifiable disease and Mr Kenneth Clarke, Minister for Health, was quoted in *The Times* as saying that 'we have no intention of dealing with AIDS patients generally under greater restraints than other patients'. (*The Times*, 21 February 1985.) However, on 16 September city magistrates in Manchester ordered the detention of a local man, suspected of carrying the AIDS virus, after he had indicated a wish to leave Mansall Isolation Hospital. (*The Times*, 16 September 1985.) The order was granted for three weeks' detention, but on 23 September a High Court judge lifted it on appeal.

But with the exception of cases involving highly dangerous diseases, where other lives may be at risk, a patient is not obliged to undergo therapy or surgery unwillingly without the sanction of the legal process. This point is very different to the alleged distinction between the physician who administers a lethal dose and one who authorises the cessation of life-sustaining therapy in situations other than hopeless.

Veatch (1978, p. 116–17) cites a borderline example of the

right to refuse treatment which cannot be deemed to be equivalent to the right to assisted suicide. Mrs Carmen Martinez was a 72-year-old Cuban woman, living in Florida, who, in June 1971, was dying of hemolytic anaemia. This disease destroys the body's red blood cells. Although a cure was not possible in this case, death could be postponed by a process of continual blood transfusion. But to facilitate the blood transfer, the patient's veins had to be opened surgically by a process known by doctors as 'cutdowns'. This was a painful and unpleasant process and she begged the doctors 'Please don't torture me any more.' The attending physician, fearing that he could be charged with aiding her suicide if her demands were met, brought the case to court where the judge ruled that Mrs Martinez was not competent to make a decision to refuse life-sustaining therapy. Her daughter was appointed her guardian and she suggested that the treatment be terminated. The court agreed that the treatment could be terminated and that this was not equivalent to granting the right to assisted suicide. The treatment was terminated and she died the next day.

What is of central importance in this case is that the decision to forego life-sustaining therapy was not taken by the physician, but that the essential aspect of the decision-making process was the patient's — or at least someone deemed confident to decide on the patient's behalf — and that under these circumstances the physician was in no way an agent of the patient's death by either commission or omission.

As long as a situation is maintained where no human being consciously and intentionally takes the life of another the slope can be avoided. However, the extent to which the right to refuse treatment can overlap with a desire for suicide can be seen in the following example.

In April 1986, a 28-year-old American woman successfully established her right to refuse therapy despite the fact that such a course was recognised as life-threatening. Elizabeth Bouvia was quadriplegic. Except for a few fingers of one hand and some slight head and facial movements she was immobile. She suffered degenerative and severely crippling arthritis. She was in continual pain. A tube permanently attached to her chest automatically dosed her with morphine which relieved some, but not all, of the pain and physical discomfort. She had previously sought the right to assisted suicide, requesting care in a public hospital whilst she intentionally starved herself to death, but the court refused her request. However, when the state of her health declined to the point where she could not be spoon fed without vomiting and nausea a drastic decision was taken. Noting the court's ruling against her suicidal intentions the hospital authorities decided that when her weight loss reached a life-threatening level a nasogastric tube should be inserted, even though it was against her will and contrary to her express written instructions.

Acting on legal advice Elizabeth Bouvia took her case to the California Court of Appeal where she sought 'the removal from her body of a nasogastric tube inserted and maintained against her will and without her consent by physicians who so placed it for the purpose of keeping her alive through involuntary forced feeding.' (Report of the California Courts of Appeal, 24 April 1986, p. 1317.)

The Court ruled in favour of Bouvia, noting that a patient has a right to refuse any medical treatment or medical service, even when such treatment is labelled 'furnishing nourishment and hydration'. This right exists even if its exercise creates a 'life threatening situation'. (Ibid., p. 1317.)

After noting similar precedents concerning the right to refuse treatment the Court cited the President's Commission for the Study of Ethical Problems in Medicine and Biomedical and Behavioural Research, which had recommended that:

> The voluntary choice of a competent and informed patient should determine whether or not life-sustaining therapy will be undertaken, just as such choices provide the basis for other decisions about medical treatment. Health care institutions and professionals should try to enhance patient's abilities to make decisions on their own behalf and to promote under-standing of the available treatment options . . . Health care professionals serve patients best by maintaining a presumption in favour of sustaining life, while recognizing that competent patients are entitled to choose to forego any treat-ments, including those that sustain life. (President's Commission, 1983, pp. 3–5.)

In keeping with these guidelines the Court ruled that Elizabeth Bouvia's decision 'to forego medical treatment or life support through mechanical means belongs to her.' It was stressed that:

> It is not a medical decision for her physicians to make.

Neither is it a legal question whose soundness is to be resolved by lawyers or judges. It is not a conditional right subject to approval by ethics committees or courts of law. It is a moral and philosophical decision that, being a competent adult, is hers alone. (Report of the California Courts of Appeal, op. cit., p. 1317.)

The question of passive euthanasia or assisted suicide was clearly ruled out when the Court stated that it was immaterial whether or not the removal of the tube caused her death. 'Being competent, she has the right to live out the remainder of her natural life in dignity and peace.' (Ibid., p. 1318.) Whether her motives were suicidal or otherwise was also considered immaterial: what mattered most was the exercise of her right to refuse therapy, not whether the motives for the exercise of this right met with someone else's approval.

In both the cases involving Mrs Martinez and Elizabeth Bouvia, providing that a physician was willing to provide treatment if required, there was no endorsement of passive euthanasia and, consequently, no danger of stepping on to the slippery slope. In cases of this kind there may even be an ethical imperative for the physician to employ all reasonable means to facilitate the continuance of treatment.

A patient who refuses treatment when expert opinion predicts inevitable death as an outcome of the refusal, may passionately hope for a miraculous recovery. From some standpoints this may sound foolish, but to override a patient's wishes in this respect would be to open the door to unwanted therapy and possible surgical assaults on unwilling victims. As Steinbock recognises, the right to refuse treatment is grounded on a different set of principles than those appealed to when the right to die is invoked.

> The right to refuse treatment is not in itself a 'right to die'; that one may choose to exercise this right even at the risk of death, or even *in order to die*, is irrelevant. The purpose of the right to refuse medical treatment is not to give persons the right to decide whether to live or die, but to protect them from the unwanted interference of others. (Steinbock, 1983, p. 291.)

It is often the case that the physician and the patient hold conflicting opinions with regard to the continuation of therapy. In cases where the patient opts for the discontinuation of therapy the physician has an obligation to put forward the case in favour of continuation as strongly as possible, but the final decision must rest with the patient.

It should be clear that little of what has been said above on the right to refuse treatment has any bearing on the alleged distinction between active and passive euthanasia. For the most part this distinction is a piece of philosophical nonsense, and physicians who take refuge behind this distinction when authorising passive euthanasia are treading on a very dangerous slippery slope. The difference between the consequences arising out of the administration of a lethal dose to an infant suffering from Down's syndrome and the consequences of witholding surgical procedures necessary for its survival rests on a line which is extremely hard to maintain. An omission when one has a clear imperative to act is a step towards the acceptance of euthanasia or even homicide. To consider an example taken from outside of medical practice: if a fire brigade sat and played cards whilst victims burnt, this would be regarded as a serious misdemeanour, which could place the firemen in a similar moral category to the arsonist who had started the fire. Certain individuals, by virtue of their competence and authority, have a greater moral responsibility for their inactions than others. But this responsibility does not extend to situations which are deemed hopeless. For here the analogy would be between the fire brigade who held back in the knowledge that a futile rescue bid was beyond the range of their equipment and with the physician who authorises the suspension of useless therapy. In such cases a great deal would depend on the definitions of 'hopeless' and 'useless', which would in turn be bound up with professional competence and experience. If nothing can be gained by intervention there is no moral imperative to intervene, and consequently non-intervention is not, in such cases, equivalent to passive euthanasia.

There are, however, serious borderline cases involving decisions to withdraw therapy from hopelessly incurable infants. With reference to treatment options for anencephalics or infants suffering from intra-cranial bleeding Kuhse and Singer advocate euthanasia, rather than a protracted dying process after the withdrawal of treatment, on the grounds that any extension of such lives could have no possible benefit.

Prolonging the life of an infant without a brain does the infant no good because it is not possible for the infant to benefit from the additional period of life. This is not, however, a medical judgement. It is, quite obviously, a 'non-medical considera-tion' based on the judgement that the handicap — in this case, the virtual absence of the brain — 'makes a person's life not worth living.' (Kuhse and Singer, 1985, p. 29.)

In some cases of this sort the withdrawal of therapy could involve a prolonged and unpleasant dying process, whereas the continuance of therapy seems only to prolong a life of suffering. Of course, a great deal turns on the severity of the handicap and the range of the therapy available. For non-medical judgements like 'unlikely to benefit' are inherently vague. Nevertheless, some conditions are so 'demonstrably awful' that death must be seen as a 'merciful release'. Yet even in these cases the departure from principle should be closely monitored.

Living wills and natural death acts

Although the right to refuse medical intervention can be regarded as an essential human right, serious borderline problems can occur with regard to situations where a person is not competent to make a rational decision. There is a widespread fear of painful death in institutional isolation in circumstances where the disease process has severely limited the ability to make decisions concerning treat-ment options. A great deal of support for voluntary euthanasia societies is generated out of concern about the loss of ability to direct care at the end of one's life. This has led to a number of religious, caring professional groups to promulgate documents usually referred to as 'living wills'. A living will is a document upon which individuals can indicate in advance a preference not to be given 'heroic' or 'extraordinary' forms of treatment to prolong life.

Many versions of living wills have been proposed. Some include a list of illnesses and disease processes which a person would not wish to suffer in his or her final days. (See Appendix I.) Others are couched in more general language, referring to 'life-sustaining procedures which would serve only to artificially prolong the dying processs'. (President's Commission, 1983, p. 39.) One New York group had distributed millions of living wills and an American newspaper columnist reported tens of thousands of requests every time she deals with the subject (ibid., p. 140). Yet despite this massive popularity the legal force of living wills is uncertain, largely because of their dubious moral status. To date there has been little or no statutory authorisation for them.

According to the Report of the President's Commission, (1983) the legal uncertainty with regard to living wills is related to the following five problems: (1) it is uncertain whether health-care personnel are required to carry out the terms of a living will; (2) those, who in goodwill, carry out the instructions of a living will may not be immune from civil or criminal prosecution; (3) there are no penalties for the destruction, concealment, or forgery, of living wills, which leaves them open to considerable abuse; (4) there is the problem of whether, in certain circumstances, the discontinuation of life-sustaining therapy is the same as active manslaughter; (5) the question of whether the cessation of life-sustaining therapy, in accord with the directives of a living will, constitutes suicide or manslaughter has not been resolved. (This latter question raises particular problems regarding insurance implications where a patient dies as a result of a physician witholding treatment.)

Nevertheless, despite their dubious legality, living wills do have some effect. If, for example, a physician were threatened with legal proceedings for witholding certain forms of therapy, the living will could be cited as part of the assessment of evidence concerning the patient's known wishes when competent. So far, despite the dubious legality of living wills no practitioner in the United States has been successfully prosecuted for having followed the provisions of a living will. On the other hand, there have been no prosecutions of physicians for not following these provisions. In the United Kingdom there has been virtually no discussion of living wills.

To overcome the uncertain legal status of living wills there have been several proposals of 'Natural Death Acts', according to which a patient may indicate a limit to treatment for certain disease processes. (See Appendix 2.) Natural Death Acts, however, are *not* facilities for euthanasia; they refer strictly to the right to remove oneself from unwanted forms of therapy. In 1976 the State of California enacted a Natural Death Act which stated that:

> In recognition of the dignity and privacy which patient's have
> a right to expect, the Legislature hereby declares that the laws
> of the State of California shall recognize the right of an adult

person to make a written directive instructing his physician to withold or withdraw life-sustaining procedures in the event of a terminal condition. (Cited by the President's Commission, 1983, p. 324.)

The act was not devised as a step towards euthanasia and expressly says so. It stresses that 'Nothing in this chapter shall be construed to condone, authorise, or approve mercy killing, or to permit any affirmative or deliberate act or omission to end life other than to permit the natural process of dying as provided in this chapter.' So far the act has not been abused: its intention is to build on the existing network of rights to refuse treatment, which are not to be confused with requests for voluntary euthanasia or assisted suicide.

California's Natural Death Act was promoted in response to widely expressed fears of loss of control over one's remaining days; it expresses a need to provide a corrective to modern medicine's tendency to give priority to *cure* over *care*. Barry Keene, Chairman of the Assembly Committee on Health for the Californian Legislature, expressed the public wish as follows:

> The development of institutionalized medicine, the emphasis on specialization and subspecialization, and the evolution of advanced therapeutic technology are antagonistic to the human needs of the terminally ill. (Keene, 1978, p. 377.)

Thus it was primarily for the restoration of dignity and control that the Natural Death Act was promoted as an opportunity to resist the infliction of technology on the dying. Reviewing the first year of the Act Keene painted a dreadful picture of death in institutional isolation, with wire meshes around the terminally ill to prevent them from committing suicide. According to Keene, the Natural Death Act is nothing more or less than an extension of the laws to enhance the application of the doctrine of informed consent at the cornerstone of the physician-patient relationship.

The Natural Death Act excludes patients in persistent vegetative states; the terminally ill new-born or child; it avoids any reference to abortion, and excludes the pregnant mother. Yet despite these exclusions the potential of the slippery slope influenced legislators, particularly over 'twilight' areas such as 'quadriplegia, retardation, senility, or other conditions of diminished brain or motor capacity'. (Keene, 1978, p. 380.) These states were excluded:

'Because of the potential for slipping into active or involuntary euthanasia based on external subjective judgements about the quality of life and without regard to well-defined medical states.' (Keene, 1978, p. 380.)

Even so, opposition to the act was fierce and its exponents were likened to Nazis. One opposition handbill contained the inscriptions: 'Long live Hitler, Kill the Aged, Weak and Poor', and went on to describe the act as the 'Legal Murder Act'. And at the Senate Judiciary Committee on 17 August 1976, opponents of the act placed a copy of W. Shirer's *The Rise and Fall of The Third Reich* at the front of the witness table. (Keene, 1978, p. 386.)

The basis of these objections were further anticipated steps down a slope towards euthanasia. But in reply the act's defenders stressed its voluntary nature, and the fact that it referred to a 'medically well-defined category of individuals who are going to die shortly . . . The decision is not even whether someone should die, but how'. (Keene, 1978, p. 381.) And as a further precaution against the slope the act contains a provision declaring its outright opposition to all forms of euthanasia.

These safeguards against abuse indicate the degree to which serious legislators recognise the force of the slope argument. For in this respect the slope argument concentrates the minds of reformers on some of the significant moral issues raised by a new proposal. Were it not for the slippery slope argument — if it were rejected as an invalid argument — then the consequences would involve the loss of the imperative to scrutinise every proposal for its moral implications. In this respect to abandon the slope argument would be to reject ethical inquiry and debate in favour of hedonism and simplistic utilitarianism.

California's Natural Death Act was immediately followed by similar statutes in at least 30 states and the District of Columbia, all of which formally establish the requirements for a 'directive to physicians' to forego life-sustaining therapy. (See Appendix 2.) Two basic problems are raised by these acts.

(1) These acts differ widely in their approach to penalties for failing to act in accord with the directive. There are also differences in their method of dealing with physicians who disagree with the directive and then fail to transfer a patient to someone who will act in accord with the directive. It is not clear whether these failures amount to a criminal or a civil offence, or whether they are deemed to be cases of 'unprofessional conduct' to be handled by the internal procedures of the relevant professional

bodies. Some statutes actually fail to address this issue at all. It is simply assumed that facilities will exist for relatives to sue for breach of contract.

(2) In addition to the legal ambiguities in current natural death acts there is very serious ethical concern over the problem of reconsideration. A decision taken during the fullness of health may merit reconsideration after the experience of illness. It is one thing to specify directives when healthy, but one may come to feel very differently when facing the finality of death. What provisions do these natural death acts have for those occasions when a patient might be deemed to have changed his or her mind? Some statutes have attempted to provide patients with adequate opportunities for reconsideration. This takes the form of the imposition of a waiting period between the time when a patient decides that further treatment is unwanted and the time when the directive becomes effective. For example, certain safeguards have been built into the California statute, according to which the provision of the act are only binding if the document is signed by a 'qualified patient'. For these purposes a 'qualified patient' is technically defined as someone who has been diagnosed as being in a 'terminal condition'. This condition is further defined as an 'incurable' condition where death is 'imminent' regardless of the life-sustaining procedures used. (President's Commission, 1983, p. 142.) But even here further safeguards are considered necessary. Following a diagnosis which meets the criteria for a 'terminal condition' the patient must wait a further 14 days after being informed of the diagnosis. Thus in order to sign the directive the patient must, it would seem, have undergone a miraculous recovery or have been mistakenly diagnosed as being in a state where death is 'imminent'. The stringent restrictions on qualification for the provisions of the act are indicative of the safeguards necessary to prevent a slippery slope towards euthanasia, where the line between involuntary euthanasia and a patient's right to refuse treatment may be blurred. It may be the case that with the help of numerous safeguards a point to halt on the slippery slope can be found. But the bewildering array of brakes required may defeat the very point of the proposal. According to the President's Commission, a study of Californian physicians, conducted one year after the law was enacted, found that only about half the patients diagnosed as terminally ill remained conscious for 14 days. Yet the statute clearly states that when a directive is required the patient must be fully *competent* and not *overwhelmed* by the disease.

Unless further confusion is to be generated, and if the slippery slope is to be avoided, then terms like 'competent', 'imminent', 'terminal', 'extraordinary', and 'overwhelmed' will have to be clearly defined and appropriate criteria for diagnosing these states clearly set out. As the Commission point out:

> There is an inherent tension between ensuring that dying patients have a means of expressing their wishes about treatment termination before they are overcome by incompetence and ensuring that people do not make binding choices about treatment on the basis of hypothetical rather than real facts about their illness and the dying process. (President's Commission, 1983, pp. 142–3.)

But the essential problem is that these statutes have to be drawn so tightly to avoid abuse that they may be of little value. On the other hand, if they are drawn up any looser they will certainly be open to various abuses. Thus the Californian Natural Death Act, which was inspired in part by the situation of Ms Karen Quinlan, would not have been applicable in her case. It should be stressed that at the time in 1975, when her father sought legal means to have Ms Quinlan removed from 'extraordinary care' procedures, including the respirator, she was not in a 'terminal condition', as defined by the Californian Natural Death Act, but in a persistent vegetative state. According to Dr Richard Beresford's assessment of legislative strategies concerning the patients in persistent vegetative states, some three years after the Karen Quinlan case:

> The current Californian Law requires not only a formal written statement by a person, while competent, that he or she does not want 'life-sustaining procedures' if a 'terminal condition' eventuates, but also evidence that death is imminent but for the life-support measures. The evidence in the *Quinlan* case did not clearly establish that death was imminent but for the use of the respirator. (Beresford, 1978, p. 343; see also Korein, 1978, p. 320.)

In a comment on the act, A. M. Capron has said:

> The only patients covered by this statute are those on the edge of death *despite the doctor's efforts*. The very people for whom the greatest concern is expressed about a prolonged

and undignified dying process are unaffected by the statute because their deaths are not imminent. (Capron, 1978, p. 55.)

The very need to maintain a distinction between the directives of a natural death act and requests for assisted suicide have, in the opinion of several critics, negated the original intentions of the legislation. Heinz (1986) points out that the qualifying state of 'terminal illness' applies only to

. . . those cases where the condition of the patient is so bad that 'regardless of the application of 'life-sustaining procedures', death would result. In such instances one does not need a Living Will to shore up one's decision to withold or withdraw 'life-sustaining' procedures. (Heinz, 1986, p. 103.)

As Capron points out, the statute's requirement 'that 14 days pass between diagnosis of imminent death and signing of a directive renders the category of "qualified patients" a vanishingly small one — only if a miracle occurs will the patient live long enough to sign a directive that will be binding.' (Capron, 1978, p. 55.)

Other problems raised by these acts involve the restrictions placed on the witnesses to the patient's decision. To avoid abuse from those who may have an ulterior motive in the termination of therapy the patient's relatives, or those concerned with the payment of the treatment, are prohibited from acting as witnesses; a situation which, in many cases, excludes from the process those whose involvement may be essential to the patient's well-being.

Perhaps these alleged weaknesses of natural death acts are themselves indicative of the significance of slippery slope objections, which entail a demand that every imaginable safeguard should be incorporated into proposals for accelerated death.

7

Beneficient Euthanasia

According to Philippa Foot, euthanasia should not be considered unless it is, in some sense, beneficial to the patient. (Foot, 1979.) As long as this principle is maintained, so the argument goes, there is no danger of a slide into a callous disregard for human life. As an advocate for beneficient euthanasia, Kohl is obliged to counter the slope objection that this would open the door to the killing of the crippled, the aged, and those who are a burden on the community and the public purse. (Kohl, 1974, pp. 96–7.) He therefore appeals to a conceptual distinction between beneficient euthanasia on the one hand and the kind of killing which was characteristic of the Nazi euthanasia programme. This narrows down to a further distinction between 'killing out of kindness' (beneficient euthanasia) and the 'kindest way of killing' (a morally weaker form of euthanasia). Quite obviously, if one is to kill it is better to do it kindly. But this does not suggest that killing kindly is just. One might embark on an evil programme of killing and still do it kindly. Killing out of kindness is clearly a different matter. There is no way in which the Nazi programme could be seen as one of killing out of kindness, argues Kohl, since it was a paradigm of cruelty, although some defenders of the overall Nazi ideology may have practised the art of killing kindly. But Kohl is concerned that many opponents of beneficient euthanasia believe that ultimately all advocacy of euthanasia rests on principles of social utility. It is for this reason that he goes to great lengths to distinguish between killing out of kindness and killing to eliminate various forms of human misery.

It must be stressed that Kohl's advocacy of beneficient euthanasia has none of the cost-benefit assumptions that often accompany requests for the legalisation of forms of accelerated death: 'The reduction of ethical principles to matters of economics generates fear and warrants the parade of Nazi horrors.' (Kohl, 1974, p. 99.) In this respect Kohl's rejection of 'fiscal utilitarianism' is beyond criticism and therefore would apparently satisfy slope objections.

We shall return to the arguments concerning fiscal utilitarianism, but this is the point at which questions have to be raised regarding Kohl's distinction between 'beneficient euthanasia' and what he sees as the 'less desirable and immoral' fiscal euthanasia programme. For Kohl does not adequately demonstrate how the fiscal utilitarian programme can be prevented from sliding through the net under the guise of a 'killing out of kindness' programme.

Now, one form of the slope argument asserts that killing out of mercy leads to an increase in other forms of killing, not because of any logical necessity of the kind envisaged by Alexander (1949), but because of the possibility of empirical confusion — naive or deliberate — between one form of killing and another. For those who want to kill for one reason may either be mistaken or rationalise the act of killing with justificatory appeals based on another reason. Those who want to kill a social nuisance might say that it was for his or her own good. A life-sentenced criminal or an elderly dependent, might come to believe that he or she would be better off dead. Could we be sure that the wish for death in such a case is not because of a desire on the part of others to be rid of a nuisance? No doubt there is less moral revulsion towards the notion of mercy killing than other forms of killing, but how do we disentangle motives? As Lady Summerskill pointed out when the House of Lords rejected the Voluntary Euthanasia Bill of 1969, 'undoubtedly there will be someone to remind the invalid of his newly-acquired powers over his own disposal.' (Cited by Lamb and Easton, 1982, p. 21.)

In this respect, the point of the slope argument is to demonstrate the practical difficulties in maintaining conceptual distinctions when reasoning with loose concepts. By drawing attention to the distinction between 'fiscal' and 'beneficient' euthanasia, Kohl has not refuted the slope argument; he has only pointed to a distinction which his opponents would acknowledge. The problem is that of demonstrating conclusively how the distinction can be maintained in practice.

But even if Kohl can deal adequately with slope predictions of further abuse, there are other slope objections, based on logical grounds which have also been made against beneficient euthanasia. In a reply to Kohl, Dyck has pointed out that:

> In dealing with the wedge argument, Kohl has not yet confronted it in its most powerful form. A wedge argument does not have to predict that certain practices will follow from another. A wedge argument is concerned with the form or logic of moral justifications. (Dyck, 1975, p. 120.)

To appreciate Dyck's objections we have to examine Kohl's paradigm case of beneficient euthanasia: a child severely-handicapped, not suffering pain, but nevertheless in a serious and irremedial physical condition which arouses in others a wish to help. In such a case, argues Kohl, induced death would probably be considered an act of kindness by most people. But, as Dyck points out, the logical objections which the slope argument raises is that even in this case it is difficult to draw the boundary of the category of beneficient euthanasia. In the foregoing example it would appear that Kohl's criterion is based on the preservation of the dignity of human beings. In Kohl's case this applied to a child born without limbs, sight, hearing, or a functioning cerebral cortex. Although not in pain and not dying, it would nevertheless meet Kohl's criteria. But, as Dyck points out, some have argued that severe cases of Down's Syndrome, however happy or educable, are also lacking in human dignity, so that they too, it would seem, could meet Kohl's criteria. Where, exactly, is the line to be drawn? This problem has certain similarities with the problem of empirical confusion, but Dyck's point goes further; it is that the slope objection reveals that there can be no clear and unambiguous means of restricting a category once a category for the authorised killing of one person by another has been accepted. Unlike arguments in favour of killing in self-defence, which deal with a very limited range of situations, the arguments for beneficient euthanasia by virtue of their reliance on abstractions such as 'human dignity', can extend to an indefinite number of cases and the reasons for restricting them are not likely to achieve universal assent. As Dyck points out:

> What the wedge argument is saying is that there is no logical or easily agreed upon reason why the range of cases would be restricted to Kohl's paradigm or why it would not be beneficial

to extend the range even beyond the retarded. For example, we have instances where quadriplegics who are fully conscious and rational are not asked whether they wish to live but are drugged and deprived of life support so that they die. The justification of this is logically the same justification for beneficient euthanasia in the case of the severely retarded. The physician considers the life of the quadriplegic to be undignified or one of suffering or, at least, a life not worth living. Such physicians certainly see themselves as acting out of kindness. (Dyck, 1975, p. 121.)

The problems entailed in the determination of a dignified death have recently surfaced in the Netherlands where euthanasia is widely practised. Yet despite the fact that 6,000 performances of euthanasia take place each year in the Netherlands and 80 per cent of the Dutch population approve of it there is still considerable opposition. One of the largest political parties, the Christian Democrats, remain firmly opposed to it lest it lead to 'a Godless slippery slope to the wanton dumping of the aged and the infirm.' (Cited by Levy in the *Daily Mail*, 29 April 1987.)

Dr Pieter Admiraal, of Delft General Hospital, who performs voluntary euthanasia by means of a lethal injection, maintains that death in these cases is beneficial, not as a response to pain, which can be largely eliminated, but as an alternative to 'a complete loss of human dignity and suffering that comes from so many other conditions such as growths that choke, constant thirst, unbearable itching and . . . a thousand things that make people lose their dignity'. (Ibid.)

It is clear that the intention behind Dr Admiraal's programme is beneficial and that it might be seen as a paradigm case of killing out of kindness in Kohl's sense. Whether it will lead to more widespread forms of killing is something we shall know about in the future. But the very indeterminateness of concepts such as 'loss of dignity' may give rise to radical reinterpretarions beyond the current programme envisaged by Dr Admiraal. Moreover, it may be significant to draw a distinction between a Nazi's motive for killing and the programme of beneficient euthanasia advocated by Kohl and practised by Dr Admiraal. But it is not merely a question of whether one person is kinder than another; there are problems as to what shall *count* as an act of kindness, and what shall constitute a meaningful and dignified life, such that its loss generates an acceptable motive for killing. Here we can have widespread differences of opinion and belief, which may be influenced by philosophical or theological assumptions concerning the concept of a dignified and meaningful life. Kohl's and Admiraal's principle of killing only out of kindness, based on a concept of human dignity, does not avoid the slope despite their humanitarian motives. Its logical implications are extensive — even if they do not reach all the way to genocide. To take an example: suppose one took as a criterion for beneficient euthanasia the minimising of suffering. Then there would be the problems raised by the possibility that killing may lead to a situation where it rules out the possibility of alternative forms of alleviating suffering, such as the provision of companionship or long-term care. (See Dyck, 1975, p. 121.) In this respect the slope objection functions in order to prevent the ruling out of other means of alleviating suffering. It is invoked in this context because it is believed that once killing becomes an acceptable way of alleviating suffering, this could lead to a retraction of other means. Even if the logical implications of tying killing to the alleviation of suffering went no further than intended by the original proposal, this could still give scope for the objection that a request for beneficient euthanasia is a protest against inadequate care.

One of the important contributions of the hospice movement has been the way that it has demonstrated how, with correct management of terminal illness, the case for euthanasia is made redundant. Cicely Saunders, the founder of the hospice movement, records a meeting with a supporter of euthanasia. She says:

> I have had much correspondence with the former chairman of the Euthanasia Society of Great Britain, and took him round St. Joseph's after I had been working there some eighteen months. He came away saying, 'I didn't know you could do it. If all patients died something like this, we could disband the Society.' And he added, 'I'd like to come and die in your home.' I do not believe in taking deliberate steps to end a patient's life — *but then, I do not get asked.* If you can relieve a patient's pain and you can make him feel like a wanted person, which he is, then you are not going to be asked about euthanasia . . . I think that euthanasia is an admission of defeat, and a totally negative approach. One should be working to see that it is not needed. (Saunders, 1971, pp. 118 – 19.)

For Saunders the hospice movement offers an alternative means of dealing with suffering other than killing patients. Now it may be the case that dilemmas of this kind are never so sharply presented. But the point behind Saunders's remarks are that if, even under the most ethically acceptable circumstances, we resort to killing, we will have taken steps which may divert us from the search for alternatives.

Now Kohl does not wish to minimise suffering by a resort to killing. He only advocates killing out of kindness. But the logical implications of killing out of kindness are much wider than he envisages, and the link between killing and kindness may easily close off other options. For Kohl, beneficient euthanasia is a last resort. This is also the criterion employed by Dr Admiraal in Holland: 'It gives me satisfaction that I have never had to say to a suffering patient, "I can do nothing for you." There is always something, this something, as a last resort.' [Cited by Levy in the *Daily Mail*, 29 April 1987.] But if there were a general policy of beneficient euthanasia, with government approval, actual practice might well be different. Last resorts, when legalised and sanctioned by cost-conscious governments, have a habit of becoming first options. Not necessarily because killing is always contagious, but because the concept of a life not worth living is open to numerous interpretations. And this is the implicit value of the parade of Nazi atrocities. Even in a society where Nazism is universally condemned, the concept of a life that is not worth living is unbounded.

8

Cost-Benefit Arguments

The paradigm case advanced by cost-benefit exponents of euthanasia is of a 'person who wants to go on living, but the cost of keeping him alive is so great that letting him die is the lesser of evils'. (Tooley, 1979, p. 71.) This type of case, although individually distressing, argues Tooley, 'is not morally objectionable'. (Tooley, 1979, p. 73.) In fact, Tooley argues that it is not even 'controversial' since 'there are limited resources available for saving lives, and if the cost of keeping a person alive is too great, one will be able to save more lives either by diverting the resources to other patients or to medical research'. (Ibid.)

This argument must be rejected whenever it appears. First, it presupposes that a fixed sum is available and no wider influx of resources is possible. Second, it lends support to the socially divisive doctrine that wealthy people should live longer. Against the first presupposition it must be observed that from its inception medicine has been short of funds. If it were to have cut its cloth according to its size there would never have been enough revenue to finance even one hospital. The second presupposition raises the wider issue of social justice in medicine. It shall not be dealt with here, except to point out that inequality of access to medical care on whatever grounds and however widely it is practised, is morally abhorrent.

A rather interesting convert to cost-benefit arguments for the termination of treatment was a former Archbishop of Canterbury, Dr Donald Coggan. In a lecture in which he referred to the escalating costs of healthcare Coggan expressed his concern over the 1975–6 United Kingdom Health Budget of £4,564 million. His remarks offer a revealing insight into the cost-benefit approach to medical care. 'The resources of the national exchequer are not limitless', stated Coggan, 'and the prolongation of the life of one aged patient may in fact entail the deprivation of aid to others and even the shortening of their lives'. (Coggan, 1977, pp. 58–9.) This, of course, is a fairly commonly held view, which nevertheless assumes a fixed level of revenue for health and often entails a belief that the only scope for resource options is within competing branches of health care — as opposed to the choice of options between the development of guided missiles and the design of artificial limbs. Then, having outlined the Church's opposition to legalised euthanasia and its possible abuses, Coggan continued to express his concern with the escalating cost of health care:

> But the awareness of these appalling abuses must not blind us to the realities of a situation the severity of which will not diminish but rather increase as the percentage of old people rises and, quite possibly, the extent of Government financial aid reaches a figure beyond which it cannot go. (Ibid., p. 59.)

Having recognised a very serious problem Coggan then revealed how easy it is, once moral imperatives are replaced by economic calculations, to slide down a slope which begins with admitting a limit to the imperative to provide health care and proceeds via concepts of social utility to the replacement of moral reasoning by economic dogma.

> The doctor has a responsibility — an accountability — to the patient and the patient's family under his immediate care. But he also has a further responsibility — to the Government or, to put it more personally but none the less accurately, to his fellow taxpayers who provide the resources to keep the National Health Service going. (Coggan, 1977, p. 59.)

It is worth noting in this passage how the ethical decisions are swiftly reduced to economic considerations. Now it is perfectly true that economic considerations feature highly in ethical problems regarding the allocation of health resources. And there is no doubt that they will continue as health care costs escalate. But in a very important sense they are irrelevant to the moral obligation to provide the utmost care for each individual. Economic considerations do not, and should not, provide the limits to moral discourse. To base one's ethical principles on fiscal criteria, or to accept fiscal limitations as the governing framework within which moral problems can be resolved, is to miss the whole point about moral commitment. To be sure, fiscal limitations do constitute a kind of reality which imposes restrictions upon the scope of possible action, but reality is not confined to economics, and does not rule out actions which are motivated by ethical ideals.

There is a scene in the film, *Gone With the Wind*, of a physician desperately trying to cope with thousands of casualties from the American Civil War. The resources are minimal in relation to the need. In fact there is virtually nothing he can do, and he knows it. But he persists, driving himself to the limit and beyond. This is a familiar phenomenon in major catastrophes. What makes it ethically significant is that the limitations imposed by the reality of the situation are only peripheral to the moral imperative to care for the sick and the dying.

Economic reality is not the kind of limit that should be compared with other limits, like the inevitability of ageing, or of parts eventually wearing out. Nor should it be compared with the kind of restraints which ethical heroes have ignored when they have disregarded the consequences of acting on a moral imperative. In an important sense it rests on a matter of political choice. The sum of £10 billion or £20 billion is not an ultimate reality; it can be provided by means of a reallocation of other resources through an act of political will.

Now it must be conceded that an individual physician is powerless against the reality of limited resources. But these limitations do not wholly coincide with ethical responsibility. It is a feature of reality that living conditions in Britain's inner cities are intolerable for those at the lower end of the social spectrum. But that is not a reason for accepting this state of affairs. It is not the task of moral philosophers and irresponsible theologians to alleviate moral anxiety with references to economic reality. It is not their task to alleviate moral anxiety at all. It is not irrational to feel personal failure when our actions are circumscribed by financial restraints. Otherwise we could not explain why a hospital, starved of funds, will become demoralised and the staff exhibit a sense of personal moral failure. Here the moral responsibility takes on a personal dimension which is distinct from an objective economic situation.

There is, of course, a great need for a redistribution of moral responsibility. Both politicians and the public they allegedly represent must be shown to bear a heavy responsibility for the neglect of health care. To be sure, on a day-to-day basis the physicians and nursing staff have to make decisions within existing resources, and for those decisions they are morally responsible. But this does not make the moral responsibility exclusively theirs — even though it is in the very nature of moral responsibility that it will be experienced in a personal sense. Philosophers and theologians who formulate their principles and ethical guidelines within the scope of available resources are, in effect, little more than unwitting spokesmen for irresponsible and morally insensitive governments.

Cost-benefit arguments often appear as significantly important side issues which, nevertheless, may hasten a euthanasia programme down a slippery slope towards more unacceptable forms of killing. In this respect it is important to keep a clear distinction between a request for the discontinuation of treatment from a patient whose decision is based on a perception of the futility of the treatment from a decision based on the actual cost of treatment. It is surprising to note how often these two situations are confused.

In a paper related to the ethical problems involved in organ transplants, Harold de Wolf refers to 'extreme measures used by physicians in hospitals to extend the half-life of people reduced to a level of existence worse than death'. (de Wolf, 1973, p. 38.) He then runs together an argument for a dignified death with proposals for terminating a life on the bases of cost-benefit considerations:

> These measures may often be paid by survivors who have not ordered them and cannot afford them. The dying man may have provided carefully to arrange for a decent income to support his widow when he was gone. Yet now the base of that income and the means of support for her meaningful life is used up in the heaping of indignation and pain upon him only for the unwanted prolongation of his dying. (de Wolf, 1973, p. 38.)

This problem is clearly a genuine one, but it is, nevertheless, a side issue in the argument as to whether or not one *ought* to extend a person's life. Changes in the social and economic structure could well remove the financial burden from the individual's shoulders, leaving the issue of whether the treatment should continue to be settled by some other means. There are grounds for arguing that a health system which places decisions of this kind on the dying is iniquitous. The redirection of a fraction of warfare expenditure towards welfare, or a change of attitude towards dependents in favour of a more collectivist standpoint, would eliminate cost-benefit considerations — although the tremendous moral problem of whether to preserve life at all costs would still remain.

9

In Vitro Fertilisation, Genetic Engineering, and the Slippery Slope

Techniques of *in vitro* fertilisation (IVF) have brought hope and the possibility of happiness for many infertile people. Yet there has been serious ethical objection to this practice. In so far as the opponents of IVF have employed versions of the slope or wedge argument it will be the concern of this chapter to focus primarily on the status of these objections.

One application of the slope agument against IVF rests on a prediction of further assaults on marriage, the family, and the related social structure. The most cited reason is the potential for IVF to separate sexual activity from reproduction. The problem with this objection is that it falsely identifies IVF as the crucial step on the slope. For the separation of sex and reproduction was far greater enhanced by the provision of more reliable means of contraception, which was, in itself, a response to a cultural demand for greater individual control over reproduction. If this is to be seen as a slippery slope towards a transformation of certain institutions, then the employment of IVF techniques, it would seem, is too late to have any significance. Whether or not methods of oral contraception over the past 20 years have been responsible for a massive social change, involving a re-evaluation of the family, is an interesting question in its own right. The point is that there is sufficient evidence to show that the social change cited by exponents of the slope argument had begun long before the development of IVF. One might say that the slope began with the separation of sex from reproduction, which took place a long time ago. In this case the slope argument would have been better employed against the earliest pioneers of family planning. Moreover, IVF is hardly likely to replace normal sexual-based reproduction which, for the most part, is more fun, can be done at home, requires no hospitalisation or surgery, and is inexpensive. It may be that the erosion of the family is imminent, but IVF cannot be said to be the crucial factor.

Many other slope objections to IVF and genetic engineering can be dismissed on similar grounds; namely, that there are more feasible alternatives for reaching the postulated end stage of the slope. This can be seen in a brief survey of the arguments for and against certain aspects of genetic engineering.

One predicted consequence of genetic engineering is the frequently cited possibility of cloning identical human beings. Suddenly the nightmare previously confined to science fiction is seen to be a possibility. Among the foreseen developments in genetic engineering are opportunities for spare-part surgery. At present the problem with organ transplants is that the recipient's immune system tends to reject the new organ. In some extreme cases the healthy transplant can even turn on the host. But with the possibility of cloning, it is held, the problem of rejection may be resolved. One proposal might be the creation of a clone for everyone, remove its brain, and keep it in a state of suspended animation in a bank for spare-parts. A transplant from a donor of this sort would be like a graft taken from an identical twin. The possibility of unlimited organ transplants is certainly attractive, and raises the possibility of rolling back the frontier of death quite dramatically. So much for the positive side. But exponents of the slippery slope argument might draw attention to some of the morally unpalatable consequences of cloning.

One of the side effects of cloning could be the creation of a whole race of slave-like clones. According to Cherfas:

> Coupled with the explosive increase in test-tube baby know how, genetic engineering has the potential to create a vast army of identical clones, each produced to some preset specification. Cannon fodder, scientists, opera singers — all could be manufactured to order if the effort that went into putting men on the moon were directed to this new form of exploration, and if we knew which, if any, genes were involved — a much greater obstacle. (Cherfas, 1982, p. 231.)

This is an example of a possible end-stage of a slope that begins with test-tube baby research and genetic engineering. Yet it does not serve as a case of meaningful employment of the slippery slope argument. There are two reasons for disqualifying this example. The first is that the end stages must be predictable factual possibilities, not dependent upon the relatively far off solutions to technical and theoretical problems which are prohibitively expensive. Given the current state of scientific ideas Cherfas does not see any immediate likelihood of cloning on a significant scale.

> The spectre of swarming hordes of clones, built to the whim of a deranged dictator, frightens; but actually it needn't. I doubt that it would be even worthwhile as an exercise, even if it were possible, which is also in doubt. We are so profoundly ignorant of the ways in which the genome finally gets expressed in a working body that we couldn't even begin to alter the genome in any major way. Single genes, yes; but reconstituting the blueprint to get a different sort of machine is likely to remain beyond us. (Cherfas, 1982, p. 231.)

But even if the technical and theoretical obstacles could be overcome, the second reason for rejecting the application of slope objections to cloning is that any postulated first step on the slope must bear the indication that the end stage will be reached primarily by the avenues made possible by the implementation of the new proposal. In short, the slope argument becomes redundant if we are already committed to the end stage by some other more available means. In the case in point, there are much easier methods of reaching the end stage. Says Cherfas:

> We could grow a race of giants, say, by tinkering with growth hormones. This has already been done with sheep, who have been induced to manufacture antibodies to their own anti-growth hormone and thereby end up twice the size of their unaltered siblings. So we could engineer human giants tomorrow, and perhaps even clone them; but the prospect of genetically engineered zombies, eager to do their master's bidding, doesn't worry me at all. The existing methods of brain-washing and mind control already do that and more, as the devastating effects of the new cults testify. With simple technologies like these at your disposal, why bother with genetic engineering? (Cherfas, 1982, p. 231.)

The slope, which invokes the spectre of cloned zombies, is one which is all too familiar in the twentieth century. Long before the issue of genetic engineering was linked to the prospects of absolute political control, the behaviourist, J. B. Watson made similar predictions.

> Give me a dozen healthy infants, well formed and my own specified world to bring them up in and I'll guarantee to take anyone at random and train him to become any type of specialist I might select — doctor, lawyer, artist, merchant-chief and, yes, even beggarman and thief, regardless of his talents, penchants, tendencies, abilities, vocations, and race of his ancestors. (Watson, 1924, p. 104.)

Genetic engineering, no more than Watson's behaviour conditioning programmes, is no match for the methods of social conditioning already demonstrated with terrifying results this century, from the mindless obedience exhibited at the Nuremberg rallies to the devastating psychological control exercised by some of the new cults, as seen in the mass suicide in 1979 at Jonestown, Guiana. (See Lamb, 1979.)

To the chagrin of many philosophers it must be said that contemporary philosophy has little to say about the early stages of human life, the status of an embryo or foetus. Philosophers' formulations of concepts of 'person', 'self', 'human being' and so on, are rarely formulated in a manner which could contribute to ethical deliberations about the status of an embryo or foetus, for they are abstruse to the point of only having a meaning within certain philosophy text-books. This, no doubt, functions as a guide in the identification of certain philosophical schools. But philosophical arguments regarding the nature of 'personhood', 'self-hood', or 'humanity' are unlikely to achieve any degree of consensus that will be of value in reaching decisions about treatment options or research proposals concerning embryos and foetuses. So instead of the usual parade of theories about personhood, selfhood, and affective qualities, the inquiry here will be based on the assumption (central to the slope argument) that all life (both human and non-human) has a moral value; not because of any actual or potential qualities, but simply because it is worth living. There are, of course, many accounts of the relative moral significance of human and non-human embryos, and of different degrees of moral recognition for the embryo, and the fully developed organism. But the point to stress is that the embryo, as an instance of life, falls within the scope of moral significance.

The major ethical problem about IVF concerns the status of the embryo. In this context the slope argument focuses on the erosion of the value of life. A successful IVF programme requires a surplus of fertilised eggs. What should be the fate of these unwanted eggs? Should they be destroyed? Or, as some argue, should they be used for experimental research? Kass (1983) presents the following slope objection to *in vitro* research, projecting the following three stages.

(1) The laboratory growth of embryos well beyond the blasto-cyst stage, including the possibility of various mammals as hosts for human embryos. Further, laboratories stocked with living embryos at various stages of development.

(2) Experiments to alter the cellular and genetic composition of embryos, various forms of genetic manipulation, including the formation of hybrids, cloning, etc.

(3) Storage and banking of embryos and ova; possibly on a commercial basis.

Against these possibilities it might be argued that future possible abuses do not disqualify present uses; that there is no certainty that position A will necessarily lead to position B. But, as Kass points out, such a line of criticism often misses the point:

> *First*, critics often misunderstood the wedge argument. The wedge argument is not primarily an argument for prediction, that A *will* lead to B, say on the strength of the empirical analysis of precedent and an appraisal of the likely direction of present research. It is primarily an argument about the *logic* of justification. Do the principles of justification *now* used to justify the current research proposal already justified *in advance* the further developments. (Kass, 1983, p. 352.)

On these terms the slope argument draws attention to the follow-ing question: How far do the principles, which underlie the pro-posed action, extend to future possibilities? Should it, for example, support the use of *in vitro* fertilisation to enable a married couple, suitably counselled, to have 'a child of their own', or should it be considered as a general form of treatment for involun-tary infertility? If IVF falls into the latter category would proper treatment methods endorse the use of *any* available technical means (to produce a healthy child) which would include surrogate wombs and even ectogenesis? By raising these issues the exponent of the slope argument forces his protagonist into a consideration of a wider range of morally relevant issues.

An illustrative analogy with current proposals for IVF is the nineteenth-century legislation permitting animal experimentation. The terms and conditions under which that legislation originally permitted certain forms of animal experimentations has been stretched beyond recognition. There is every possibility that, unless it is carefully scrutinised, legislation regarding IVF may be in the same situation in 100 years time, with legislators equally incapable of acting. There is, however, an important caveat to make here: it may be the case that every possible folly cannot be legislated against. But there is a moral imperative to try. For as Kass warns 'once the genies let the babies into the bottle, it may be impossible to get them out again'. (Kass, 1983, p. 353.)

According to Kass it is important to examine the *scope* of justification provided by the principles governing a new proposal. On these terms a moral assessment of proposals for IVF research and experiments on human embryos should not begin with questions regarding the morality or immorality of these proposals but rather with an attempt to 'understand fully the meaning and significance of the proposed action'. (Kass, 1983, p. 344.) This concern with the significance of IVF proposals transcends benefit or harm to those concerned. It is, says Kass, bound up with 'a whole range of implications including many that are tied up with definitely foreseeable consequences of this research and its predictable extensions — and touching even our common conception of humanity'. (Kass, 1983, pp. 344–5.)

The ethical appraisal of research proposals should extend to the foreseen possibilities within the scope of the principles applicable to that research programme. It is therefore ethically inadmissible not to consider the slippery slope in any research proposal. In the case of IVF proposals the ethical issue is not merely the risk of bodily harm to the human subjects concerned, or of the benefits bestowed upon the infertile. There is a risk of moral harm which extends beyond the immediate issues. According to Kass: 'At stake is the *idea* of the *humanness* of our human life and the meaning of our embodiment, our sexual being, and our relations to our ancestors and descendants.' (Kass, 1983, p. 345.) For Kass, the end-stages of the slope indicate a slide towards a loss of respect for human life.

At this point it might be objected that the slope argument rests on a confusion between a blastocyst and a person; that while a blastocyst may be a potential person it is no more a person than an acorn is an oak tree. Consequently there is no case for endowing the embryo with the rights that are bestowed upon persons, and that the use of embryos for experimental research is not a step in the direction of harmful research on persons.

The foregoing objection, however, misses the point of the slope argument. For it need not be maintained that an *in vitro* blastocyst has a right to life, or that interference with it constitutes a form of assault similar to assault on a person. The point is that, as a piece of living tissue, a blastocyst is entitled to some of the respect due to a living being. Says Kass:

> But the blastocyst is not nothing; it is *at least* potential humanity, and as such it elicits, or ought to elicit, our feelings of awe and respect. In the blastocyst, even in the zygote, we face a mysterious and awesome power, a power governed by an immanent plan that may produce an undisputably and fully human being. It deserves our respect not because it has rights or claims or sentience (which it does not have at this stage), but because of what it is, now *and* prospectively. (Kass, 1983, p. 346.)

There are, of course, different forms of respect due to both embryos and to fully developed human beings. Merely because something does not fulfil criteria for the full status of humanness or personhood does not mean that it is merely a thing. As Veatch points out:

> An embryo, human or otherwise, should not be treated capriciously. A human embryo is human in biological form even if it lacks the crucial integration of the mental with the organic. It deserves respect at least because of the emphatic links it has with the moral community, both in its biological form and in the potential it possesses. Such embryos should not be disposed of without good reason. By extension they are already part of the moral community. (Veatch, 1984, p. 247.)

On these terms an embryo deserves some, though not all, of the respect due to a member of a moral community. However, just as a seed should not be confused with a plant, so the moral standing of an embryo should not be confused with the moral standing of a child. Although it may be immoral to dispose of an embryo in a cavalier manner, on Veatch's terms the moral status of an embryo is not sufficient for it to have a right to life. Says Veatch:

> But prior to the accrual of full moral standing that comes with the linking of the mental and the physical, the moral prohibition against killing does not apply. (Veatch, 1984, p. 247.)

It might be objected that Veatch has placed too much emphasis on the requirement of mental and physical unification. One possible objection might be that various forms of dementia or anencephaly might be seen to be excluded from the 'moral prohibition against killing'. Some qualification is obviously required. It is this: only a being without any brain function at all at either end-point of existence — can be excluded from moral prohibitions against killing. Strictly speaking, of course, a being without any brain function is not alive and cannot be killed. What would be destroyed is tissue, not human life in any sense. Nevertheless, Veatch's essential point still holds: even tissue is entitled to some degree of moral significance. For this reason post-mortems are considered as a violation of the human body, and have to be justified on the basis of more pressing moral criteria, such as suspicion of serious crimes, professional negligence, or with attempts to save other lives. For if they are performed for trivial reasons they reveal a lack of respect for the being for whom that body was its corporeal home.

The different levels of respect due to embryos and persons can be recognised more clearly if we compare a miscarriage with the death of a human being. When the loss of a foetus in miscarriage is mourned, sympathy is usually directed at the woman who has miscarried. It is *her* loss, *her* miscarriage. We do not institute burial and mourning facilities for a miscarriage as we would after the death of an infant. An embryo or a foetus is not entitled to the same recognition of its demise as a human being. Nevertheless, if it were proposed that we ate discarded embryos as a 'great delicacy' — a form of human caviar — there is no doubt that the human blastocyst would be protected by our taboo against cannibalism, which insists that human flesh, albeit the flesh of the dead, is not used as meat. '*The human embryo*', says Kass, '*is not mere meat; it is not just stuff; it is not a thing. Because of its origin and because of its capacity, it commands a higher respect.*' (Kass, 1983, p. 347.)

Although the embryo is not entitled to the same respect as a fully developed being it is still entitled to respect. To deny this is to weaken the value of life. The question is: How much respect is due to an embryo? Kass proposes that it is equal in status to a more developed foetus; that the early embryo *in vitro* is analogous to the early embryo in *utero*, since both are potentially viable. Consequently, restraints imposed on early embryo research should be the same as those on foetal research. (Ibid., p. 347.) This might seem excessively scrupulous but there is no other point at which a line can be drawn without stepping on the slope.

An objection to this view might consist in pointing out that an *in vitro* blastocyst has less resemblance to the more mature form than a living foetus. But 'look-alike' qualities have little bearing on the issue of whether or not a being is entitled to human respect. Victims of explosions, massive burns, or severely deformed infants, may not be adequate look-alikes, but they are not regarded as mere meat.

There is, nevertheless, an important caveat to the proposal that embryos should be treated as members of a moral community: whilst it is argued that embryos, like foetuses, are entitled to membership of a moral community, this does not necessarily guarantee their right to life. In controversies over the manipulative and experimental research on embryos it is the loss of respect for living tissue rather than the loss of life which justifies the slippery slope argument.

If Kass's argument is correct, then the answer to our initial question — What should happen to the surplus fertilised eggs? — is that we should let them die if there is no chance of implantation. Experiments on them should be prohibited in line with the prohibition of experiments on aborted foetuses and human corpses where prior permission from the deceased has not been given. On these terms if the being in question does not have the opportunity to authorise the disposal of his or her remains then experimentation is unwarranted and immoral.

Attempts to rebut the slippery slope objection to research on embryos focuses jointly on the alleged inevitability of the slope and on the postulation of acceptable criteria to limit abuses. In a reply to Kass, Samuel Gorowitz argues that finding a means of stopping on a slippery slope is simply a matter of skill. 'Fortunately, it is possible to start down a slippery slope and then to stop.' (Gorowitz, p. 356.) The legalisation of voluntary terminated pregnancies, he argues, has not led to infanticide because we have a clear idea when to stop. The problem with this example is that the legalisation of voluntary terminated pregnancy was not a step on the slope in the first place. It was advocated as an *alternative* to infanticide, not as a path in that direction.

According to Gorowitz the point at which experimentation should be prohibited is with the onset of sentience in foetal development. (Gorowitz, 1983, p. 361.) This, as he correctly points out, marks a qualitative difference in the status of the foetus. The problem with Gorowitz's position is that he appears to confuse the plea for moral respect for an embryo with a plea for specific human rights. Now a sentient being may well have rights that are not possessed by the non-sentient: it may have the right to reply to an argument, the right to be addressed by its correct name, for example. But the possession of sentience does not account for a being's entire moral status. A fully developed sentient human being may have rights that a fully grown lettuce does not possess. And it is intuitively obvious that a lettuce seed has no inherent rights in the normal sense. But even something as trivial as a lettuce seed may fall within the scope of ethical significance. A good gardener may take pride in caring for and nurturing seeds and developing plants; they have a plan which is awesome and deserving of respect. There was a time when philosophical reflection began with a feeling of awe and respect for the world; nowadays the non-sentient world, including non-sentient humans, are perceived as mere things and the awe and wonder about the most simple aspects of nature are dismissed as lacking utilitarian significance. But like a seed, or plant, which in contemplation is awesome, an embryo human or otherwise is an entity of moral significance, although not entitled to the *same* kind of respect as that accorded to a sentient being. One cannot after all embarrass, insult, or apologise to a non-sentient being, but these aspects are only partial manifestations of moral concern.

A more significant line of criticism of Kass's position would be to question his concept of 'respect', which is inadequately presented. In what sense is a human embryo entitled to more respect than other objects which have been accorded respect although used for experimental purposes? Human cadavers are legitimate objects of respect but they can, under closely controlled circumstances, be used in experimental research. It would seem that, under similar conditions, embryos used in research could still be treated with respect. It might even be argued that it is partly the awe and respect felt about an embryo that motivates research on it. For it is precisely that awesome potential of an embryo to become a fully developed organism that makes it an attractive subject for research. As Gorowitz notes with regard to experiments on human embryos, 'it is the blastocyst's potential to become a human being that makes it an object of particular research interest'. (Gorowitz, 1983, p. 361.) In one research application during the the 1970s the United States government Ethics Advisory Board ruled that it was ethically acceptable for the applicant, Dr Soupart, to study non-human embryos as long as they were not kept alive beyond two weeks. Dr Soupart's reply indicates the manner in which the moral status of living embryos can be recognised. 'I only asked for a week', he said, 'they gave me an extra one, which I honestly don't know what to do with. I have the greatest respect for every embryo I look at.' (Cited by Taylor Fleming, 1983, p. 399.)

Many researchers have echoed Dr Soupart's sentiments, and it would seem that research on living embryos is not incompatible with retaining their moral significance. The following passage contains the kind of wonder and admiration that an embryo can elicit.

> An embryo has an extraordinary thrust towards life. In a warm room at Johns Hopkins University, Dr Yu-Chik Hsu keeps mouse embryos alive in incubators for half of their 19-day gestation period to study the cause of malformation and congenital disease. On the eighth day, their hearts begin to beat, hard; to the unassisted eye, they look like tiny pulsing polka dots of life. (Taylor Fleming, 1983, p. 399.)

Even the limited imaginations of utilitarian philosophers can comprehend the fact that respect is due to these microscopic entities. But if we grant this we still have the problem of distinguishing such cases from the respect due to fully developed beings. To resolve this problem it will be necessary to articulate more fully the concept of respect. A distinction between 'strong' and 'weak' respect may be helpful in this context. Strong respect would be the kind of respect shown to fully developed animals, both human and non-human, which is bound up with the full array of obligations and rights of fully developed human beings, some of which can be extended to cover the moral status of non-human animals. Weak respect, on the other hand, would correspond to the respect or reverence, shown to ex-persons, cadavers, amputated limbs, organs, removed tissues, miscarried foetuses, embryos and blastocysts. Although the latter can be disposed of as things they are still accorded a moral significance in that they have characteristics associated with living beings. Whether forms of weak respect are due to the bodies and tissues of non-human animals, however, is very much dependent upon the degree to which a culture affords them a degree of strong respect in their fully developed state. Consequently, under adequate saeguards akin to those which protect other forms of human issue, there is no danger of stepping on to a slope with regard to research proposals on embryos. Providing existing sanctions are adequately applied with regard to their use there need not be any prohibitive fears of future abuse. Of course other objections to *in vitro* research may prove to be conclusive but there are no grounds to fear that present research proposals will lead to a decline in the value of living beings — although some of the philosophical justifications of this research may well exhibit a loss of value.

10

Voluntary Termination of Pregnancy and the Slippery Slope

One of the most central questions in the debate over the voluntary termination of pregnancy is, 'When does human life begin?' Unlike the question, 'When does human life end?', which has a clear cut answer in terms of the 'loss of integrated functioning of the organism as a whole' at which point the person is no more, the problem of an absolute beginning does not yield much certainty. There is not a specific moment, or time, when we can clearly indicate the presence of human life or personhood. When determining the end points of human life or personhood there are conceptual guidelines, such as brain death, which yield clinical criteria (Lamb, 1985), and which can be objectively determined. But when determining the beginnings of human life there is little consensus about these very guidelines. Until that is achieved the problem of an objectively·determined beginning to life will remain insoluble.

Attempts have been made to locate the beginning of human life at various intra-uterine stages. It is with reference to the difficulty of defining such a precise and morally significant moment in the gestation process that the slippery slope argument enters into ethical discussions on the voluntary termination of pregnancy.

According to Joel Rudinow, the 'extreme conservative' position with regard to the voluntary termination of pregnancy is one which locates the beginnings of human life at the moment of conception. As such the argument employed by conceptionists is a version of the slope argument, which Rudinow presents as follows:

> Birth is a morally insignificant event in the history of the born individual. As far as personhood and entitlement to treatment from the moral point of view are concerned, birth, which for

the body is a mere change of the environment, is no more significant than the first birthday. But once birth has been demythologized, as well it should be, we are on a slippery slope. For no particular point between birth and conception is a point at which the person/non-person distinction can be non-arbitrarily located, because the difference in development between any two successive intra-uterine points are so unimpressive. Consequently, we are forced to locate the beginning of human life at the point of conception. (Rudinow, 1974, pp. 173–4.)

According to Rudinow, the problem with the conservative position is that it blurs the distinction between zygotes and persons. This is undoubtedly correct. But Rudinow's mistake lies in thinking that it is the conservative's employment of the slope argument that is responsible for the confusion. (Lindsay, 1974, p. 32.) On the contrary, the slope argument in this context should not be taken to imply that human life begins at conception; it is simply directed against a position which makes a claim on behalf of any significant moment in the gestation process. If the conceptionist employs the slope argument to support the idea that the point at which life begins is conception, then he or she is drawing from the argument something which is not in it. We can find an example of this illicit use of the slope argument in Norman St John Stevas's argument that since there is no qualitative difference between the embryo at the moment of conception and the moment of quickening, the embryo must be considered a human being. (Stevas, 1963, p. 32.) The reply to this argument is that a foetus is no more a person than an acorn is an oak tree, and that the killing of an acorn is not the same as killing a tree. However, this reply only corrects a mistaken application of the slope argument, which is not a defence of conceptionism but rather a means of drawing attention to both empirical and logical difficulties in the maintenance of conceptual boundaries around definitions of significant and insignificant life. Nevertheless, unless it is settled decisively what shall count as a human being, it is impossible to predict that liberal attitudes towards voluntarily terminated pregnancy will lead down a slippery slope towards forms of abuse. If, as the slope argument maintains, there is no significant event which marks the beginning of life, then there is no Rubicon to be crossed during embryological development upon which we can concentrate and say, 'Before this moment we have an object as trivial as a nail paring; after this we have an individual human being to which we must reserve the full sanctity of human life.' (Potts, 1969, pp. 74–5.) As long as the entity is given respect due to human tissue — which need not entail the preservation of its existence — then respectful disposal is acceptable. Unless we have an idea of what it is we are disposing of, then we cannot say that we are on a slippery slope. In the case of voluntary terminated pregnancies the slope argument only applies to human beings or cases when a foetus would be seen as a human being. In this respect the prohibitions on voluntary termination of pregnancy may be perfectly compatible with doctrines which have no regard for the right to life. The Nazis outlawed voluntarily terminated pregnancies and even made it a capital offence. 'It was', as Malcolm Potts says, 'the philosophy that produced concentration camps that also carried out the last European execution for abortion.' (Potts, 1969, p. 75.)

Yet in one very important sense the ethical issues surrounding voluntarily induced termination of pregnancy are distinct from the factual question, 'When does human life begin?' This is a biological matter which, if it can be determined as precisely as the end-point of human life, should be kept apart from questions concerning how living beings are to be disposed of. More central to the issue of voluntary terminated pregnancy are decisions as to whether or not one is morally responsible for the maintenance of another life, the degrees of responsibility held by parents, and the economic and material conditions which may have a bearing on the decision not to continue with a pregnancy. To this discussion the slippery slope argument has little to contribute, since decisions regarding responsibility to other lives have long been considered in other contexts.

It was argued in Chapter 2 that a limited case can be made for retaining the analogy between Nazi practices and certain contemporary practices in the context of recent developments in the biomedical sciences. It must be stressed, however, that the liberalisation of laws regarding voluntary termination of pregnancy does not have any analogy with medical practices under the Nazis. Abortion was illegal for German nationals and did not appear in their proposals for *Rassenhygiene*, since euthanasia and sterilisation were considered to be the best methods.

Nevertheless, certain techniques presently available do suggest a possible analogy between contemporary proposals for pregnancy termination and the Nazi experience. Amniocentesis now allows foetal cells to be examined for certain kinds of genetic disorders. This service is performed by physicians in a context where there is a willingness to terminate a pregnancy whose outcome is generally known to be genetically unsatisfactory. Furthermore, among research successes usually cited in discussions of certain diseases is the ability to detect the disease at an early state, when the prospective parents can decide whether to continue with the pregnancy. At present amniocentesis is a voluntary procedure. But it is very easy to imagine a situation where the continuation of the existing social pressure to give birth only to healthy offspring may lead to a situation where it is a non-voluntary, even mandatory, procedure. The slope argument can be seen in the question asked by Margaret Steinfels:

> Will it become so unusual for a baby to be born with Down's Syndrome that there will be no support or sympathy for a family with such a child? Society will say, 'Well, you've chosen this. You live with the consequences of having brought such a child into the world.' (Steinfels, 1976, p. 16.)

This development certainly does not conform with the racist aspects of the Nazi ideology, but it does indicate the strength of a concept of human purity.

One important aspect of the slippery slope argument, as we have seen, is the fact that new policies, introduced on a voluntary basis, have a habit of becoming mandatory. Family planning was first defended under the banner of 'individual choice', often against entrenched opposition. Once it was established it was deemed to be a voluntary matter; one had a free choice with regard to the size of one's family. But there is a peculiar tendency about certain kind of reforms by which a liberalising motive gives way to an authoritarian compulsion. In the case of family planning what next emerged was a concept of a responsible free choice. Nowadays only a minority would agree that between eight and twelve offspring was an example of a responsible and free choice. Consensus has settled in favour of limiting progeny to small families and those who opt for larger numbers are often deemed irresponsible. In similar contexts we can see the relevance of slippery slope objections to many liberalising measures. For it is necessary to guard against a tendency to transcend the boundaries of voluntary actions towards their becoming mandatory; from the liberalisation of voluntary terminated pregnancies to a situation where social pressure may oblige prospective parents to accept involuntary termination.

At present there is an emerging consensus that would endorse the voluntary termination of pregnancy when the outcome would be affected by haemophilia or Down's Syndrome. One can certainly appreciate the moral motives behind such proposals. But once we have introduced the concept of a life that is not worth sustaining, the slope argument, with its attendant borderline problems, must be taken into consideration. Suppose the boundaries of permissible termination are drawn to include Galactosemia? This is a disease that causes mental retardation, yet it can be treated fairly simply by keeping the child off milk. Since it can be detected pre-natally we could present the parent with a decision whether to terminate. It might be pointed out that with adequate care the child would be perfectly normal. But the parents might well prefer a termination on the grounds that it would be a nuisance, saying that 'we can always try again'. It is this kind of borderline case that makes the slope argument appear relevant to the ethical problems of voluntary induced termination of pregnancy.

11

Conclusion

The force of the slippery slope argument is not so much in its appeal to the moral superiority of the *status quo*, although it does serve as a warning against the difficulties of maintaining newly proposed boundaries. In the absence of absolute knowledge and consequently absolute control over the consequences of our actions and decisions, we cannot afford to ignore the possible misuses of proposed reforms. Philosophers live in a world of clear-cut distinctions, where conceptual boundaries are easily identified. The real world, however, does not conform to such idealisations — although such distinctions may be a necessary means of coping with the world. When exponents of the slippery slope argument appeal to the indeterminateness of certain concepts they draw attention to an aspect of truth and reality which may be obscured by those seeking to impose clear-cut distinctions upon the world. Truth is not always to be identified with rational distinctions between concepts, but is found in their necessary interpenetration. Thus terms and expressions like 'voluntary', 'involuntary', 'curable', 'incurable', 'rational desire' and 'irrational desire' all earmark sharp distinctions, yet on close examination it is hard to retain their absolute distinctness. For this reason, when facing moral reform, the slippery slope argument is a reminder of the elasticity of certain concepts.

The value of the slippery slope appeal can be seen in Veatch's objections to the killing of the dying, where an analogy between the universal prescription against killing the dying and the universal adoption of the red light traffic rule is drawn. (Veatch, 1978, p. 97.) It may not be necessary to stop at every red traffic light. It may even be advisable to break the red light rule, say in an

120

emergency when no car or pedestrian is present. In order to allow for these circumstances it might be preferable to adopt a weakened version of the red light traffic rule: 'Stop at every red light unless the road is clear and you have very sound reasons for ignoring it.' But the problems with this rule is that it is inherently unclear, lending itself to numerous interpretations and possible accidents. It would multiply mistakes, generate misunderstanding, and create numerous borderline instances. Exactly what is a 'sound reason' for ignoring the red light would itself create tremendous misunderstanding. It is therefore preferable to follow the existing rule, however inefficient it may appear at times. This situation is similar to proposals for accelerated death. The significance of the slope argument is in the way it reveals the inherent, but frequently overlooked, problems entailed in proposals to redraft the rules in order to accommodate what are currently regarded as ethically justifiable breaches of it. Under the present laws a wise judge will display leniency towards a driver who breaks the red light rule in order to prevent a catastrophe. So would a wise judge exhibit leniency when dealing with a case of accelerated death if there was overwhelming evidence that the killing was based on merciful intentions. This requires no change in the law and maintains a situation in which the onus is very much on those who wish to accelerate death to provide the justification for their actions. If life has an absolute value then moral deliberations about particular lives should also rest on a presumption in favour of life. The citing of exceptional cases where euthanasia might be morally defensible is no argument for a change in the law or for a re-drafting of our attitudes towards life. In such cases the law is best maintained, but with leniency and understanding.

Appendix 1
Living Will Declarations

Concern about loss of ability to direct care during the end stages of life, or with the onset of certain non-recoverable diseases has led various caring organisations to promulgate documents known as 'Living Wills', according to which an individual can specify directives concerning treatment options prior to the onset of a disabilitating condition. At present their legal status is uncertain and there are no clear cut legal guidelines for health-care personnel confronted with a living will. The following declaration is typical of living wills distributed by various euthanasia societies in the United States.

(This example is distributed by the Society for the Right to Die and is dated March 1986.)

LIVING WILL DECLARATION

To My Family, Doctors, and All Those Concerned with My Care

I, _____, being of sound mind, make this statement as a directive to be followed if for any reason I become unable to participate in decisions regarding my medical care.

I direct that life-sustaining procedures should be withheld or withdrawn if I have an illness, disease or injury, or experience extreme mental deterioration, such that there is no reasonable expectation of recovering or regaining a meaningful quality of life.

These life-sustaining procedures that may be withheld or withdrawn include, but are not limited to:

SURGERY   ANTIBIOTICS   CARDIAC RESUSCITATION
RESPIRATORY SUPPORT
ARTIFICIALLY ADMINISTERED FEEDING AND FLUIDS

I further direct that treatment be limited to comfort measures only, even if they shorten my life.

You may delete any provision above by drawing a line through it and adding your initials.

Other personal instructions:

These directions express my legal right to refuse treatment. Therefore, I expect my family, doctors, and all those concerned with my care to regard themselves as legally and morally bound to act in accord with my wishes, and in so doing to be free from any liability for having followed my directions.

Signed _____ Date _____

Witness _____ Witness _____

PROXY DESIGNATION CLAUSE

If you wish, you may use this section to designate someone to make treatment decisions if you are unable to do so. Your Living Will Declaration will be in effect even if you have not designated a proxy.

I authorize the following person to implement my Living Will Declaration by accepting, refusing and/or making decisions about treatment and hospitalization:

Name_____

Address _____

If the person I have named above is unable to act on my behalf, I authorize the following person to do so:

Name_____

Address _____

I have discussed my wishes with these persons and trust their judgement on my behalf.

Signed_____ Date_____

Witness _____ Witness _____

(Another example of a living will. This one is dated 1972 and was distributed by the Euthanasia Educational Council of the United States of America.)

THE LIVING WILL

TO MY FAMILY, PHYSICIAN, MY CLERGYMEN, MY LAWYER — If the time comes when I can no longer take part in decisions for my own future, let this statement stand as the testament of my wishes:

If there is no reasonable expectation of my recovery from physical or mental disability, I, _____ request that I be allowed to die and not be kept alive by artificial means or heroic measures. Death is as much a reality as birth, growth, maturity and old age — it is the one certainty. I do not fear death as much as I fear the indignity of deterioration, dependence and hopeless pain. I ask that drugs be mercifully administered to me for terminal suffering even if they hasten the moment of death.

This request is made after careful consideration. Although this document is not legally binding, you who care for me will, I hope, feel morally bound to follow its mandate. I recognize that it places a heavy burden of responsibility upon you, and it is with the intention of sharing that responsibility and of mitigating any feelings of guilt that this statement is made.

Signed _____

Date _____

Witnessed by:

_____

_____

Appendix 2
Natural Death Acts

The first American state to draft a Natural Death Act was California in 1976. This act contains a directive to physicians (reproduced below) which must be signed by the declarant in the presence of two witnesses not connected to the declarant by blood or marriage, and who are not entitled to any portion of the estate of the declarant upon his decease. The attending physician and those in his employ are also excluded from witnessing.

Natural Death Acts are framed with specific passages which stress that they should not be seen as steps towards either passive or active euthanasia and patients who fulfil the criteria outlined by these acts are not regarded as victims of suicide.

STATE OF CALIFORNIA
DIRECTIVE TO PHYSICIANS

Directive made this _____ day of _____ (month, year).

I _____, being of sound mind, wilfully, and voluntarily make known my desire that my life shall not be artificially prolonged under the circumstances set forth below, do hereby declare:

1. If at any time I should have an incurable injury, disease, or illness certified to be a terminal condition by two physicians, and where the application of life-sustaining procedures would serve only to artificially prolong the moment of my death and where my physician determines that my death is imminent whether or not life-sustaining procedures are utilized, I direct that such procedures be withheld or withdrawn, and that I be permitted to die naturally.

2. In the absence of my ability to give directions regarding the use of such life-sustaining procedures, it is my intention that this directive shall be honored by my family and physician(s) as the final expression of my legal right to refuse medical or surgical treatment and accept the consequences from such a refusal.

3. If I have been diagnosed as pregnant and that diagnosis is known to my physician, this directive shall have no force or effect during the course of my pregnancy.

4. I have been diagnosed and notified at least 14 days ago as having a terminal condition by _____, M.D., whose address is _____, and whose telephone number is_____. I understand that if I have not filled in the physician's name and address, it shall be presumed that I did not have a terminal condition when I made out this directive.

5. This directive shall have no force or effect five years from the date filled in above.

6. I understand the full import of this directive and I am emotionally and mentally competent to make this directive.

Signed _____

City, County and State of Residence _____

The declarant has been personally known to me and I believe him or her to be of sound mind.

Witness _____

Witness _____

Bibilography

Alexander, Leo (1949) 'Medical Science Under Dictatorship', *New England Journal of Medicine*, 14 July 1949, pp. 39–47, 241.

Beresford, Richard H. (1978) 'Cognitive Death: Differential Problems and Legal Overtones', *Annals of the New York Academy of Sciences*, 315, pp. 339–48.

Black, Max (1970) *Margins of Precision*, Cornell University Press, Ithaca, NY.

Brophy, Julia and Smart, Carol (eds.) (1985) *Women and the Law*, Routledge and Kegan Paul, London.

California Courts of Appeal (1986) *Daily Appelate Report*, 24 April.

Capron, Alexander Morgan (1978) 'The Development of Law on Human Death', *Annals of the New York Academy of Science*, 315, pp. 46–61.

Cherfas, Jeremy (1982) *Man Made Life*, Blackwell, Oxford.

Chesterton, G. K. (1937) 'Euthanasia and Murder', *American Law Review*, 8, p. 486.

Coggan, Donald (1977) 'On Dying and Dying Well', The Edwin Stevens Lecture. Extracts in *The Journal of Medical Ethics*, 3, pp. 58–9.

Dawidowicz, Lucy (1976) 'Biomedical Ethics and the Shadow of Nazism', *Hastings Center Report*, Special Supplement, August.

De Wolf, Harold, L. (1973) 'Organ Transplant as Related to Fully Human Living and Dying', in *Ethical Issues in Biology and Medicine*, edited by Preston Williams, Schenkman Publishing Company, Cambridge, Mass., pp. 33–45.

Dougherty, Charles J. (1985) 'Criteria For Morally Acceptable Research With Human Subjects', *Explorations in Medicine*, Vol. 1, No. 1, pp. 3–22.

Dyck, A. (1975) 'Beneficient Euthanasia and Benomortasia: Alternative Views of Mercy', in *Beneficient Euthanasia*, edited by M. Kohl, Prometheus Books, Buffalo, NY.

EXIT (1980) *The Last Right: The Need for Voluntary Euthanasia*, revised edition, EXIT, London.

Foot, Philippa (1979) 'Euthanasia', in *Ethical Issues relating to Life & Death*, edited by J. Ladd, Oxford University Press, New York, pp. 14–40.

Guardian (1985) 8 January.

Guardian (1985) 9 January.

Guardian (1985) 11 January.

Glover, Jonathan (1977) *Causing Death and Saving Lives*, Penguin Books, Harmondsworth.

Gorowitz, Samuel (1983) 'Progeny, Progress and Primrose Paths', in *Moral Problems in Medicine*, edited by S. Gorowitz, R. Macklin, A. L. Jameton, J. L. O'Connor, S. Sherwood, Prentice Hall, Engelwood Cliffs, NJ, pp. 355–63.

Harris, John (1985) *The Value of Life*, Routledge and Kegan Paul, London.

Heinz, Laurence (1986) 'The Right to Die and the Erosion of Patient Rights', *Hawaii Medical Journal*, Vol. 45, No. 3, April, pp. 103–7.

Independent (1987) 1 May.

Jacobovits, Sir Immanuel (1974) 'Discussion on Death and Euthanasia', CIOMS Eighth Round Table Conference, World Health Organisation, Geneva.

Kamisar, Yale (1958) 'Some Non-Religious Views Against Proposed "Mercy Killing" Legislation', *Minnesota Law Review, 42*, 969, 1030–41.

—— (1983) 'Euthanasia Legislation: Some Non-Religious Objections', in Gorowitz *et al*, (op. cit.) pp. 458–64.

Kass, Leon (1983) 'Making Babies Revisited', in *Moral Problems in Medicine*, in Gorowitz *et al*, 2nd edition, (op. cit.) pp. 344–55.

Keene, Barry (1978) 'The Natural Death Act: A Well-Baby Check-Up on its First Birthday', *New York Academy of Sciences*, Vol. 315, pp. 370–93.

Kohl, Marvin (1974) *The Morality of Killing*, Peter Owen, London.

Korein, Julius (1978). Editorial note in *New York Academy of Sciences* 315, p. 320.

Kuhse, Helga (1982) 'An Ethical Approach to IVF and ET: What Ethics is All About', in *Test Tube Babies*, edited by William A. W. Walters and Peter Singer, Oxford University Press, Melbourne, pp. 22–35.

Kuhse, Helga and Singer, Peter (1985) *Should the Baby Live?*, Oxford University Press, Oxford.

Lamb, David (1979) 'Brainwashing and Consciouness Rising', *Solidarity, 8*, May–June, pp. 14–16.

Lamb, David and Easton, S. M. (1982) 'Philosophy of Medicine in the United Kingdom', *Metamedicine*, 3, pp. 3–34.

—— (1985) *Death, Brain Death and Ethics*, Croom Helm, London.

Langer, Elinor (1983) 'Human Experimentation: New York Verdict Affirms Patients' Rights', in *Moral Problems in Medicine*, edited by Gorowitz *et al*, (op. cit.) pp. 626–32.

Levy, Geoffrey (1987) 'The Doctor Who Kills With Compassion', *The Daily Mail*, 29 April.

Lindsay, Anne (1974) 'On the Slippery Slope Again', *Analysis*, 35, pp. 32.

Maguire, Daniel (1977) 'Deciding for Yourself: The Objections', in *Ethical Issues in Death & Dying*, edited by F. Weir, Columbia University Press, New York, pp. 320–47.

Mansson, Helge Hinding (1977) 'Justifying the Final Solution', in *Ethical Issues in Death and Dying*, edited by Robert F. Weir, Columbia University Press, New York, pp. 308–19.

McCullough, Lawrence (1976) 'Biomedical Ethics and the Shadow of Nazism', Hastings Centre *Report*, Special Supplement, August.

Melrose, Diana (1982) *Bitter Pills: Medicines and the Third World Poor*, Oxfam, London.

Milgram, Stanley (1974) *Obedience to Authority*, Harper and Row, New York.

Nagel, Thomas (1979) *Mortal Questions*, Cambridge University Press, Cambridge.

Observer (1986) 3 March.

Potts, Malcolm (1969) 'The Moral Problem of Abortion', in *Biology and*

Bibliography

Ethics, edited by F. J. Ebling, Institute of Biology, London, pp. 173–6.
President's Commission for the Study of Ethical Problems in Medicine and Biomedical and Behavioural Research (1983) *Deciding to Forego Life-Sustaining Treatment*, US Government Printing Office, Washington DC.
Rachels, James (1983) 'Active and Passive Euthanasia', in *Moral Problems in Medicine*, in Gorowitz *et al.*, (op. cit.) pp. 286–9.
—— (1986) *The End of Life: Euthanasia and Morality*, Oxford University Press, Oxford.
Ramsey, Paul (1970) *The Patient as Person*, Yale University Press, New Haven, Conn.
Rudinow, Joel (1974) 'On the Slippery Slope', *Analysis*, 34, 5, pp. 173–6.
Saunders, Cecily (1971) 'The Moment of Truth: Care of the Dying Person', in *Confrontations of Death: A Book of Readings and A Suggested Method of Instruction*, edited by Francis G. Scott and Ruth M. Brewer, Oregon Center for Gerontology (A Continuing Education Book), Corvallis, Oregon.
Singer, Peter (1979) 'Unsanctifying Human Life', in *Ethical Issues Relating to Life and Death*, edited by J. Ladd, Oxford University Press, New York, pp. 41–61.
—— (1983) 'Justifying Voluntary Euthanasia', in *Ethical Issues in Modern Medicine*, edited by John Arras and Robert Hunt, pp. 210–19.
Steinbock, Bonnie (1983) 'The Intentional Termination of Life' in *Moral Problems in Medicine*, Gorowitz *et al.*, (op. cit.), pp. 290–5.
Steinfels, Margaret (1976) 'Biomedical Ethics and The Shadow of Nazism', Hastings Center *Report*, Special Supplement, August.
Stevas, St John (1963) *The Right to Life*, Hodder & Stoughton, London.
The Times (1985) 21 February.
The Times (1985) 22 March.
The Times (1985) 26 April.
The Times (1985) 16 September.
Szasz, Thomas S. (1977) 'The Ethics of Suicide', in *Ethical Issues in Death & Dying*, edited by Robert F. Weir, Columbia University Press, New York, pp. 374–86.
Taylor, Fleming, Anne (1983) 'New Frontiers in Conception: Medical Breakthroughs and Moral Dilemmas', in *Ethical Issues in Modern Medicine*, 2nd edition, edited by John Arras and Robert Hunt, Mayfield, California, pp. 397–401.
Taylor, Telford (1976). Contribution to 'Biomedical Ethics and The Shadow of Nazism', Hastings Center *Report*, Special Supplement, August.
Time (1973) 23 July.
Tooley, Michael (1979) 'Decisions To Terminate Life and the Concept of a Person', in *Ethical Issues Relating to Life and Death*, edited by John Ladd, Oxford University Press, New York, pp. 62–93.
—— (1983). Cited by Steinbock in 'The Intentional Termination of Life', in *Moral Problems in Medicine*, Gorowitz *et al.*, (op. cit.) p. 290.
Veatch, Robert M. (1978) *Death, Dying and the Biological Revolution*, Yale University Press, New Haven, Conn.
—— (1984) *A Theory of Medical Ethics*, Basic Books, New York.
Walsh, Joseph (1976) Contribution to 'Biomedical Ethics and the Shadow

of Nazism', Hastings Center *Report*, Special Supplement, August.

Watson, J. B. (1924) *Behaviourism*, Chicago University Press, Chicago.

Weiss, Sheila Faith (1983) *Race Hygiene and the Rational Management of National Efficiency: William Schallmayer and the Origins of German Eugenics 1890–1920*, Ph.D. Thesis, Johns Hopkins University, Baltimore, Maryland.

Wertham, Frederic (1980) 'The Geranium in the Window: The Euthanasia Murders', in *Death, Dying & Euthanasia*, edited by D. J. Horan and D. Mall, Aletheia Books, Maryland, pp. 602–41.

Williams, Bernard (1985) 'Which Slopes are Slippery?', *Moral Dilemmas in Modern Medicine*, edited by Michael Lockwood, Oxford University Press, Oxford, pp. 126–37.

Williams, Glanville (1967) *The Sanctity of Life and the Criminal Law*, Alfred A. Knopf, New York.

Index